AROUND THE WAVES

THE HERITAGE OF THE ISLE OF WHITHORN

Edited by
Mike Marshall

Foreword by
Jack Hunter

Breathing Space Productions
Isle of Whithorn

ISBN 978-0-9565894-0-8

© Isle News

First published by
Breathing Space Productions, Isle of Whithorn, 2010

The contributors of the articles contained in this book
have agreed that all proceeds from this publication be
paid to the Isle Futures Charity for the future funding
of creative literary and publishing projects in the area.

Photography © Michael Marshall
Archival material is also drawn from the
Isle of Whithorn Heritage collection
and other personal memorabilia

British Library Cataloguing-in-Publication Data
A catalogue record for this book is available from the British Library

Printed at the Stranraer Free Press,
St. Andrew Street, Stranraer

AROUND US THE WAVES

THE HERITAGE OF THE ISLE OF WHITHORN

CONTENTS

Before We Begin - *by Mike Marshall*

I spent the first years of my working career literally surrounded by film. The BBC's news film library was a graphic introduction for me in the importance of archiving our history – at whatever level – world, national, local. Whether it was film or stills, nothing that had been screened or had any perceptible value for future use was 'junked', to use a bit of media parlance. Over successive decades, the methods of capturing and storing information changed, sometimes at bewildering pace. But being able to refer back to imagery that showed how we lived, what we did at work, in the home, in our communities, was always a prime concern.

The autumnal night sky, looking west from the Isle. Despite the glow of street lighting in Stranraer some 30 miles away, and which has been emphasised by the time exposure, Galloway's 'Dark Skies' status is not impaired, with Ursa Major and the Plough clearly seen on the left.

Whether it's television or radio, printed media or the world-wide web, archives, communal or personal, are a precious asset. It's incumbent on every one of us to ensure that we leave a legacy of information for succeeding generations – even the most insignificant observations can grow in importance and value in the space of just a lifetime.

This book would not have been possible without a small band of people in the Isle of Whithorn whose foresight in squirreling away pictures, notes and cuttings of events, people and places in the Isle helped lay the foundation of a digitised Isle Heritage collection. In an increasingly disposable society, the preservation of such material was to prove invaluable for a good number of articles that appeared in *Isle News,* the community's quarterly magazine, as well as other projects.

Over the past ten years I've been privileged to create a collection of new photographic material of Isle events, comings and goings, seasons and activities. The encouragement given to me by the community in this very pleasant and absorbing task is greatly appreciated, and I would express my sincere thanks to everyone who has assisted me, no matter how small their contribution.

My thanks also go in no small way to Jack Hunter, who has been so supportive of heritage projects in Wigtownshire, for his inputs on St Ninian and foreword to this book, and whose highly entertaining literary contributions and skills have been an inspiration to us all.

Above all, this book is the result of the teamwork of the *Isle News* editorial committee, and the support shown over the years by our advertisers and sponsors. Prudent financial management by the team over the years has enabled this publication to come to fruition, and I am especially grateful to them for all their help, advice and perseverance over the years. I am especially pleased that any funding generated by sales will be set aside for future publishing and creative literary projects in the Isle.

Finally, a very special thank you to my ever-patient wife Jean who, as deadlines for print loomed ever closer, would provide me with restorative calming and reasoning. Her attention to administrative detail has been one of the pillars of the *Isle News* project, and of course, this book.

I hope that *'Around Us the Waves'* will be a valued source of information and a lasting reminder of a very special community and place in Scotland. Whether you are among those who are fortunate to live here, or have connections with the Isle, or maybe are just visiting and curious to find out a bit more about us - enjoy our heritage!

Foreword – *by Jack Hunter*

The title of this publication is supremely appropriate, for the story of the Isle of Whithorn has been determined by the sea. In an age of the primacy of land transport it is easy to think of the village and its hinterland as isolated and peripheral. However in the millennia before the nineteenth century railway age the main form of transport was by sea, and the Isle was close to a major national crossroads where routes to the west and east intersected with the great north-south seaway running along the west coast.

With its position and fine natural harbour, the only one in the area, it was therefore a place of importance: a seventeenth century writer described it as "a very advantageous port". As confirmation of that claim, some goods from overseas bound for the royal burgh and county town of Wigtown had to be transhipped at the Isle because of its superior harbour facilities.

From as early as the beginning of the sixth century the Isle was the port for what became the royal burgh of Whithorn and its great, prosperous, and much visited religious foundation. It is unsurprising that the area abounds in evidence of early immigrants and that village life and the local economy centred on the sea; this was a place that built ships and bred sailors.

The dominance since the nineteenth century of land transport and the Isle's marginal position in that situation have destroyed its importance in a communications context but the sea still dominates economic life here. Commercial fishing is significant; as an attractive coastal village it has tourist, leisure, and retirement appeal; and the sea's moderating influence on the climate is beneficial to local agriculture.

The Isle's maritime DNA has even proved a military advantage with the siting at Burrowhead before and during World War Two of a Royal Artillery practice camp, and which used the waters of Luce Bay as a repository for novice gunners' attempts to master the skills of firing heavy AA guns.

Around Us the Waves is a welcome celebration of this rich inheritance in its many aspects.

1 – More Than Just a View
Ian Duncanson sets the scene on this unique location

For decades visitors have come to the Isle of Whithorn to behold the picture postcard view of the harbour and graceful crescent of shore and neat houses.

But 'The Isle', as it's more usually called locally, is more than just a view. 1600 years ago this tiny community was in at the very beginning of Scotland's Christian history – when Ninian, Scotland's first missionary saint, made landfall in the area – well over a century before the much celebrated St Columba.

Traditionally, the Isle has always looked to the Solway Firth – it was the port for the town of Whithorn and much of the surrounding country. A century ago the sea was the high road in and out of these parts. A haunt for smugglers, and a principal harbour for legitimate trade and transport – here the many necessities of life would come and go – cargoes of cattle and sheep, coal, fertilizer and timber. For many, this was where a hopeful journey to the other side of the world began.

The sheltered anchorage and quay is still the main focal point of the village today – busy throughout the year with local boats fishing for crabs and lobsters, as well as catches of scallops brought in by the Manx fleet. It's a welcoming port for visiting leisure sailors to take on supplies and fuel and sample the peace and quiet.

Isle News, the community's magazine, was first published in Easter 2001, and many of the articles and features that appeared over the next nine years are the basis of this book.

Additional material has also been drawn from the community's website **www.isleofwhithorn.com** and there is also some new writing. Through *Isle News* we recorded a story of a community endeavouring to ensure, sometimes against considerable odds, that it was, and still is, an attractive and viable place in which to live and enjoy its very special character.

We started at a time of considerable adversity. A year into the new Millennium and still recovering from the *Solway Harvester* tragedy, *Isle News* was precipitated into an early birth by the first case of foot and mouth disease in the Machars. The community's new magazine found a receptive audience at a particularly dreadful period. The gradual recovery and regeneration of the Isle became a regular and important feature of the quarterly publication. A team of ten was responsible for news-gathering, writing and researching, collecting pictures, editing, preparing layouts, printing and distributing the 35 issues that were to appear. Our readership was not just local but extended worldwide to a diaspora of folk with Isle connections.

Our heritage and history; our enterprise on the land and at sea; and our encouragement of new talents and skills among all ages, together with a strong community spirit have made the Isle what it is today. It's a success story of which we should all be proud, it covers many generations, and it's a story that has only just begun.

July 2005: A Group of Isle youngsters proudly 'unveil' their newly created Post Office planter with blacksmith artist Rachel McWilliam and Councillor Alistair Geddes in attendance

Cooking up a Treat—P17

Isle News

SILENT SPRING

This is a headline which a month or so, possibly even a couple weeks ago, might have seemed out of place here in the Isle. When word of the first suspected case of foot and mouth in the Machars came to the Palm Sunday congregation, there was a gasp of dismay, almost disbelief. The news we least wanted to hear, and by that afternoon the outbreak at Sorbie had been confirmed. It's for this reason that the first edition of **Isle News** has been brought forward from May 1st. One of the purposes of the newsletter is to enable our small community to express its feelings about any matter—amongst itself, or indeed anyone who wishes to keep in touch with us in whatever way they can. Having already been elsewhere the effects on farming, all the supporting industries, and of course tourism, it's not a moment too soon to start the all-important task of assessing the scale of the problems that we are facing here.

The small editorial team that have come together to produce **Isle News** hope that in some small way this journal may help in

Our First Issue:

Because we have published this inaugural issue a fortnight early, and many residents may not yet have returned their request forms, we are distributing this *Isle News* free to every household in the Isle Community Council area. **If you haven't already done so, please remember to let us have your subscription request for future issues as soon as possible.**

Alex Currie, local Minister, h conducting an almost constant c logue by telephone with affecte ers in the community. 'In some he said 'it's very similar to just e year ago at the time of the *Solwa Harvester* tragedy. Once more we have a community in crisis. It's a when we really see people's respo at their best - everyone is rallying round. Farmers who've been affer have said to me that all the many 'phone calls they've been receiving have been extremely comforting, m cially when they really have little or no idea at what the future may now hold for them.' He went on - 'I'm deeply impressed by the way that the communities are rallying together on more - neighbours and friends are doing all they can to help farmers in whatever way they can. What is good to hear is that even though we don't know whether we're facing a total wipe-out of the industry in the Machars, people are even now beginning to talk about rebuilding. They are considering how best they can re-commit themselves, and standing together is the best way to do it'.

A disinfectant point has been installed Harbour to allay Isle of Man fears of in from Foot & Mouth disease spreading fishing fleet.

> We'd all dared to believe that we'd possibly escaped.......
>
> It's a life's work for the next generation down the drain.....
>
> You know everyone—it affects the whole area— all those lovely animals put down—when you lose your life's work like that how do you start again?
>
> We're dreading the inevitable—who knows what we'll face in two or three weeks time?
>
> Consider yourself a potential carrier of this disease....

A SENSE OF PLACE

Jack Niblock and John Scoular recently recorded a series of talks on the Isle's Maritime Heritage for the Isle Archive project. Here's a small taste of what they said

John Scoular: Most of what we learned was not just at our mothers' knee, in most cases it was at our granny's knee. There aren't so many people here left here who can trace their ancestry back to more or less at least three generations actually living in the village. Jack Niblock is, as far as I know, the solitary surviving Master Mariner in the Isle... a hundred years ago there were at least 40 people living in the village who held Master's tickets. *Jack Niblock:* In The Sailing Club there is a copy of the first chart ever made of the Isle harbour. This was made when the Isle was an island. Isle and in 1793 it shows we had a well established village - houses in re are still standing today.... the Captain's Garden, and a space which went right Port and the harbour, with all the storehouses down the harbour itself. Captain Cook was really only discovering Australia and starting to map New

ch traffic was carried by sea - we are talking about a time when it was a lot was by road. And that is why so many of us have such links with Liverpool, and the topsail schooners before her carried everything and everybody. For people here, if you wanted a job Liverpool was the place you had to go, we've still got as many relations in Liverpool as we have left here. Liverpool isn't that far away, I can vividly remember my grandmother taking me outside in the war and seeing the glow in the sky from the fires and the searchlights at Liverpool during the blitz. But even in those days it wasn't so far and the paddle steamers certainly made a very regular job of it.

(Regattas, the Isle Lifeboats, the Harbour, Shipbuilding and Shipwrecks, World War Two and Burrowhead and the Saga of the Perch - all have been recalled vividly, and these are now being made available on the History pages of the Isle's website— *www.isleofwhithorn.com* —*Ed*)

2003 COMMUNITY LIFE WINNER • CALOR

£10213
NINETY DAY WONDER!

First Response Target is reached and broken!

£7000
£6000
£5000
£4000
£3000
£2000
£1000

The Isle's First Response Team's Fund Raising efforts have produced an astonishing result—over £10,200—and all in just 90 days! That's equivalent to receiving almost

The first group of Responders after their training weekend in May

£113 per day since their campaign started at the end of February. Announcing the figure to a well-attended first Annual General Meeting of the First Response Team, Sheena Newberry said: "This is a night of celebration and one which the village should be justly proud of. First, the magnificent sum of £10,213 had been raised, doubling the original target. Second, the number of young people who had volunteered their services as Responders, eight have already been trained and a further six will go through that experience at the beginning of July." Adding that the Response Team hoped to give live this August, Sheena emphasised that all responders are trained by the Scottish Ambulance Service and undergo full Police Disclosures. They will all wear an ID card with photograph, and sweatshirt-style uniforms with the approved logo.

> To Back Page ▶

This edition of Isle News is sponsored by Burrowhead Holiday Village

---

The *Isle News* team

SCOTTISH COMMUNITY • CALOR SCOTLAND • OF THE YEAR

CALOR CROWNS THE ISLE!

The Isle's Big Day in Edinburgh — Full Reports inside

ISLE NEWS
ISLE OF WHITHORN

Issue 35 - Autumn 2009 - Price 75p

WELCOME HOME!

STOP PRESS
ONE STOP
SHOP IS GO!
See Page 12

Isle News
ISLE OF WHITHORN

BOLLARDS!

rdinary headline you may but then this is the result of a ordinary meeting to progress for the Harbour Row works. After two very productive sions with Alastair Speedie, one of loway's supremos of Environment ture, the Isle's Community Council. from Isle Futures, the Sailing Club, Row property owners, expressed and disbelief when they were preg, that the agreed area for the siting of car park in the field to the rear of the cket during the works be £8000 to breach

that she had a budget of £8000 to breach

COUNCIL GETS OUR MESSAGE
VILLAGE GREEN WILL NOT BECOME A CAR PARK!

the existing dyke opposite the slipway... remove rock outcrops undertake some minor grading to accommodate all Harbour Row facility (inten displaced by the reconstruction wo said that this did not represent be for the Council, and instead, **that the Village Green be parking.**

Councillor Alastair Geddes, chaired all the meetings, said intensely disappointed development, only a week works were due to commence the frustration of all present productive consultation with said, "there is no intention of all this work to be turned particularly close to th tourist season, with visitors able to use the harbour, and loss of business that will h the community."

Time and again the meet that at the two previou Alastair Speedie, agre reached on a strategy be renegotiated at the Chairman refused to a present agreed unanim

We got what we agreed - fencing for the temporary car parking facility is now in place

Continued on Back Page

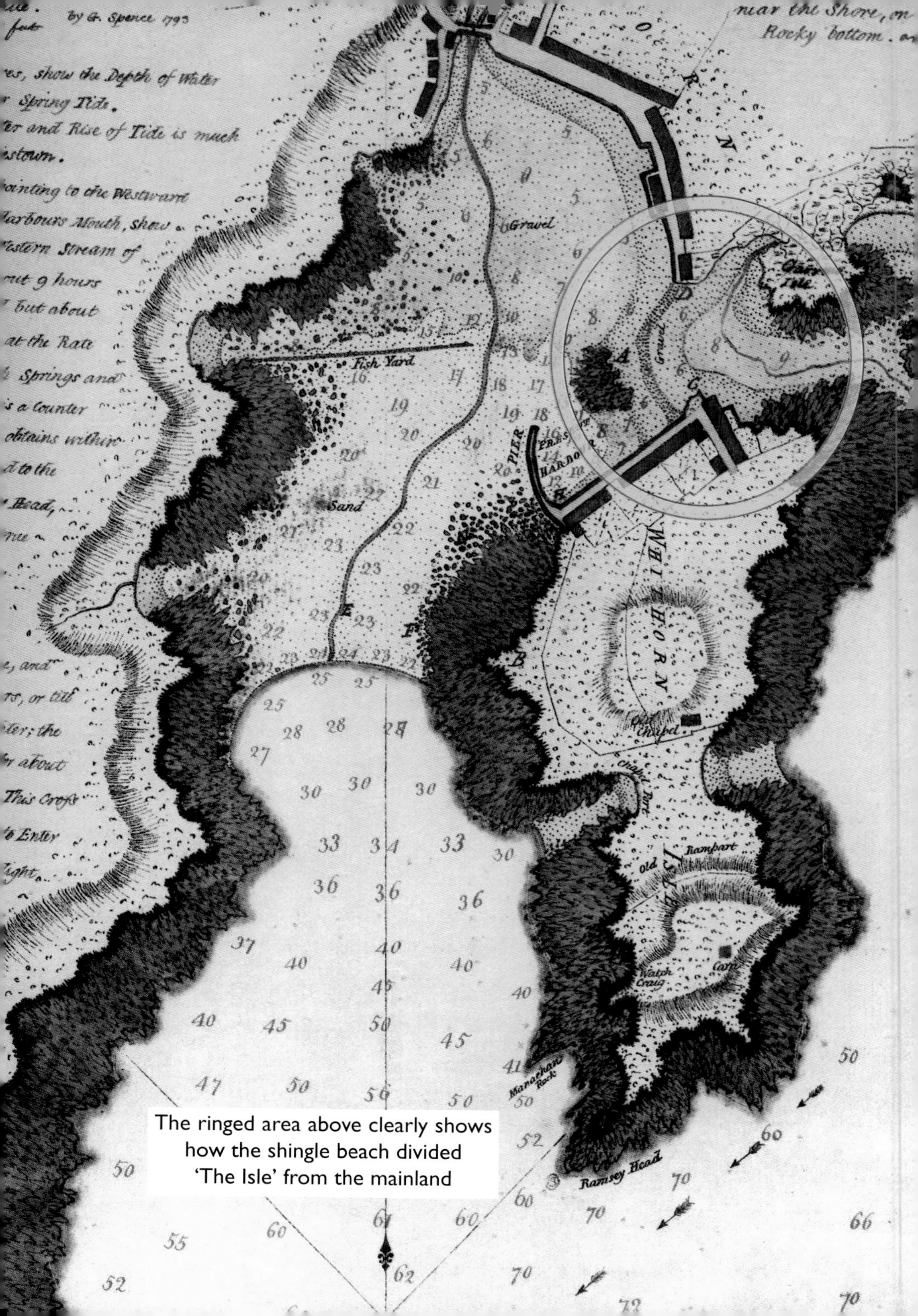

by G. Spence 1793

near the Shore, on
Rocky bottom.

...es, show the Depth of Water
Spring Tide.
...er and Rise of Tide is much
...stown.
...ointing to the Westward
...arbours Mouth, show
...stern Stream of
...it 9 hours
...t but about
at the Rate
...Springs and
...s a Counter
obtains within
...d to the
...Head,
...ue
...s, and
...s, or till
...er; the
...r about
This Cross
...to Enter
...ight,

O C E A N

Gravel

Oyster
Isle

Fish Yard

PIER
PRES
HARB.

Sand

WEI HORN

Chapel

old
Rampart

Watch
Craig

Managhan
Rock

Ramsey Head

The ringed area above clearly shows
how the shingle beach divided
'The Isle' from the mainland

2 – *Why Are We Called 'The Isle'?*

by John Scoular

First question from any visitor—and often many locals—is why the village is called the Isle of Whithorn when it is obviously and solidly connected to the mainland. Second in the query list is also always the same – what is the history of the Cairn?

The first is relatively easy to answer, particularly with one of the many good aerial shots of the village. Or more simply, looking back at the village from the Cairn, it is easy to see how close the shoreline is running up to the entry that once led to the school.

It is also relatively easy to date when a gravel beach became a causeway, complete with houses. Copies of two early charts help us pin down the dates. The first, dated 1793, is kept in the Wigtown Bay Sailing Club, together with many other artefacts of local history. This chart dates back to when the authorities were contemplating what would need to happen to make the harbour non-tidal. Nothing ever came of it, but that chart does show a shingle beach—and refers to the Isle as a separate location, with the mainland as Whithorn.

Isle of Whithorn

Received your P.P.C. safely this morning. I have got 100 now, so my collection is getting on. How are you enjoying your holidays in Glasgow.

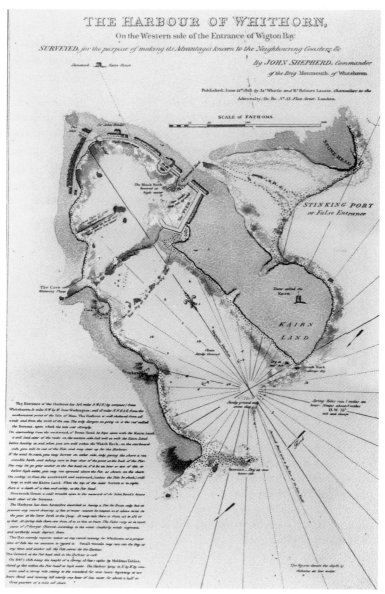

The second chart, shown above, dates from 1818 and is on view in the hall of the Steam Packet Hotel.   Reproduced above, it clearly shows houses where the tides used to meet at high water.

Of course the best story about that is probably apocryphal but none the less charming.   It tells of a smuggling vessel being pursued by the Revenue cutter into the bay.

The officers followed at their leisure thinking the smugglers were safely trapped, only to find their quarry had gone and just visible standing away to the Kirkcudbright coast. Legend has it that locals investigating at low water found a groove in the gravel where the smugglers had charged their way over. A lovely tale.

But, under extreme conditions – a south easterly gale on top of spring tides – the waters have been known to meet, as local householders are well aware. Today many believe that things have not been helped by the modern sewage works. Where high tides and heavy seas used to discharge themselves safely into what was then the school yard, the new works turn the hydraulic power of the waves back along the garden walls. Nature does not like us interfering.

The Cairn is a much more complicated story, combining history old and new. Once part of Glasserton Estate, the lands were given to the village by the then Laird, Admiral Johnston Stewart, and today are looked after by the local authority, and responsibilities are shared with both Historic Scotland and Scottish National Heritage because of its variety of treasures.

Probably the oldest traces of civilisation lie right at the top where the ditches protecting the Iron Age fort are still very visible, with the ancient agricultural system known as ridge and furrow also clearly to be seen below them.

The history of the white tower itself is not as clear as it appears only as a pile of stones on the early chart.

It later had coastguard connections and latterly the white tower was really just a day mark, allowing vessels to safely identify the entrance to the bay and harbour and not stray into the False Entry, as the Stinking Port is described on early charts.

The compass rose carved on the rocks just a few metres south of the white tower was probably done by a coastguard and is a challenge for the sharp-eyed to find.

The Cairn, Isle of Whithorn.

Also on the high ground of the Cairn are a few remnants of the World War I field gun which was once there as a War Memorial. Further west is the high point known as the Watch Craig, which commanded a panoramic view of the harbour entrance and which was once the place where a beacon could be lit as a navigation guide. Today a solar powered light on top of the white tower gives modern mariners the safe vectors for entering the bay.

A 1920's postcard showing the white tower and World War I field gun

On the seaward side of the tower, offering always a wind sheltered corner to enjoy the magnificent views, the view takes in the Carrick shore, the English coast and the Isle of Man, just twenty miles away. The concrete platform there carries the poignant memorial to the great village tragedy – the loss of the *Solway Harvester* and all its young crew in 2000.

The actual concrete base goes back to the time of the Burrowhead gunnery range.

Going back down the hill towards the village the remaining walls of the old lifeboat house – now home of a cairn of remembrance stones – lies just above the two little ports where the old pulling and sailing lifeboats were launched. The remains of the concrete slip on the west side date back only to World War II when it was built to bring ashore RAF launches involved with the anti-aircraft training at Burrowhead Camp.

A 1930's post-
card showing
the old lifeboat
house, with St.
Ninian's Chapel
in the back-
ground

Still there however – and generations have tried to lift and pull it away, is the anchor chain which was used with the block and tackle needed for launching the old lifeboat.

To the east of the remains of the old lifeboat house is St. Ninian's Chapel, the village's much visited reminder of its early Christian history. The actual origins of this building, constructed to commemorate St. Ninian's coming ashore, remain historically confused and there are traces of a much earlier structure. One for the pure scholars among us to research.

The path back to the village now leads through a popular children's play area to the harbour, but along the rocky edges are a last historic secret for the curious to look out for – the large iron rings let into the rocks so that sailing schooners could be warped in or out of the bay against the wind.

There's a mass of history on the Cairn, but for many perhaps the favourite is a childhood memory of a natural playground with many rock pools and hidey holes with colourful residents such as sea anemones, hermit crabs, shrimps and all sorts of marine life. It's something that has remained unchanged down the ages.

The white tower basks in autumn sunshine;
the navigation beacon and solar power
panel were installed in 2001; to the right is
the *Solway Harvester* memorial

3 – A Cairn With a View

Andrew MacAlpine surveys one of the Isle's best viewpoints

"And over there you can see Ireland", said the man at the Cairn to a group of walkers. Well, not quite – but, if it's not Ireland, then what can be seen from the Cairn? "Quite a lot" would really seem to be the answer.

Let's look first of all towards the harbour. Leaving out the village, which needs a whole chapter to itself, the countryside beyond reveals, on the right-hand side, a series of dairy farms. Many of

Isle Farm can easily be seen to the north

the fields are defined by immaculately maintained dry-stone dykes with the tops securely cemented in the Machars style. Furthest to the right is Isle Farm which wins for itself an entry in the Dumfries and Galloway volume of *'The Buildings of Scotland'*. The farmhouse is described as a "broad-eaved Tudor cottage orné" which, when you see how large it actually is, forces a rethink of what the term "cottage" means.

The view across the Harbour bay to Burrowhead

The dramatic cliffscape that can be seen from the coastal walk between Burrowhead and the Isle. In the distance is the white tower, with Stein Head to the left; In the far distance, across Wigtown Bay is the shore that leads to the River Dee and the entrance to Kirkcudbright harbour

To the left of the village the fields splay out towards Burrowhead. For a period in the nineteenth century the tenant of Morrach farm was obliged to maintain a unique navigational aid known as the Manxman's Compass. This was a 20-foot square of near vertical cliff which had to be painted white every other year. This operation required ropes and ladders and no doubt a good head for heights. The practice seems to have ended around 1890 when it was decided that the cliff was becoming unstable.

Moving clockwise round the Cairn, looking over the chalets of Laigh Isle, let your eye follow the line of the cliffs and across the water of Wigtown Bay to the rough shore on the Kirkcudbright side. Before the coastline disappears, the lighthouse of Little Ross Island stands out clearly. It is one of a series of lighthouses built by the remarkable Stevenson family whose most famous member was Robert Louis of 'Treasure Island' fame. It was built in 1843 for the then enormous sum of £8,000. It achieved unwanted fame in 1960 when one of the keepers was found shot dead there. His fellow keeper was arrested and convicted of his murder.

Seen from near Cutreoch, the Robin Rigg windfarm is caught in winter sunlight

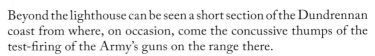

Beyond the lighthouse can be seen a short section of the Dundrennan coast from where, on occasion, come the concussive thumps of the test-firing of the Army's guns on the range there.

To the right of that stretch of coast, in the waters of the inner Solway Firth, something quite new has appeared. The Robin Rigg wind farm extends in a long line of turbines each standing 250ft high, sixty of them in all, generating enough power for more than 100,000 homes. The total cost – around £500 million.

From the south side of the tower and, with the aid of good visibility and binoculars, there comes into view a foreign land – England. This stretch of the Cumbrian coast has been called the least-known section of the English coastline, the millions of visitors coming to the Lake District largely leaving out the western side.

The three main towns of Maryport, Workington and Whitehaven show up best at night thanks to their street lights. This is an area of declining or indeed defunct heavy industry. Plentiful deposits of iron ore and coal enabled industries to be developed here in the nineteenth century. Workington once had the most advanced steelworks in the world thanks to the inventor Henry Bessemer with his revolutionary steel converter process. Whitehaven also could claim a record for the most extensive system of undersea coalmine workings in the world, stretching for miles beneath the seabed. Thousands of men were employed and millions of tons of coal extracted, but at a terrible cost with hundreds of miners killed including 117 in a single disaster in 1947. Now the steelworks and mines are closed, and the harbours through which so much was exported are being adapted to provide marinas for yachts and powerboats.

The biggest source of employment now can be seen shining in the evening sun far down the distant coast – the Sellafield nuclear facility. Its size is astonishing: the site covers four square kilometres and the workforce numbers almost 10,000.

And, just in case you thought the obvious had been omitted, there are the mountains and hills of Cumbria. For once the term glorious panorama is justified. Perhaps best seen in winter with a low sun and snow covering the tops, a whole series of fells and pikes stands out with the highest of them all, Scafell, visible. Deep clefts between the hills mark the location of hidden and lesser-known lakes such as Ennerdale Water and Wast Water. The hills finally disappear into the sea just short of Barrow-in-Furness.

All that leaves perhaps the most striking view of all. It is only 20 miles or so to the nearest landfall on the Isle of Man. There is the illusion from here of seeing the whole length of the island; in fact

The magnificent skyline of the Lake District seen early on a winter morning from the Isle

it angles away at about 45 degrees so that what you are looking at is the north-west of Man.

The two obvious peaks are North Barrule above Ramsay, and Snaefell itself which just makes it over the 2000-foot mark. On a clear day, powerful binoculars might enable you to spot the electric tram crawling its way up to the summit, and you can certainly see the headlights of cars on the mountain road at night.

A light blinks from the northernmost tip of the island. The 100-foot Stevenson lighthouse at Point of Ayre is almost two centuries old. Beside it, until it was recently decommissioned, a huge foghorn bellowed out so loudly that it could be heard here in the village.

The Isle of Man retains a link with the Isle of Whithorn with scallop fishing boats from Peel regularly calling here to discharge their catch. Just a thought – wouldn't it be rather nice if that link was developed to include a regular summer passenger service?

No view of Ireland then, but a complete 360-degree sweep that few other places on the coast can rival. Here's wishing you a clear day whenever you are at the Cairn.

Seen from the Cairn, the northwest coast of the Isle of Man. A summertime profusion of sea pinks in the foreground

This postcard from about 1905 shows the distinctive terrace of Tonderghie Row and Dunbar House with its unique 'eyebrow' windows

4 – A Choice Retreat

Early Travel Guides to the Isle surveyed by Andrew MacAlpine

> Where else is such a choice retreat,
> To rest and hear the breakers beat,
> And thus from care the mind to wile,
> As by the cairn that crowns "the Isle"?

So wrote the self-styled Bard of Galloway whose verses are to be found in *Tours of Galloway*, a guide that appeared annually from the end of the nineteenth century. The Isle was by then a recognised holiday destination. Whereas a modern guide might write of peace and quiet by the sea, the entry for the Isle in the 1900 edition of *Tours in Galloway* pulls out all the stops:

"Devoid of the gaieties and artificialities, which by the elaboration of the effort to amuse, pall upon the visitor to more frequented resorts, the 'Isle' offers as a restorative for jaded nerves a perfect tranquillity which old Neptune seasons with a health giving sea breeze." (Try saying that without drawing breath!)

The coming of the railway to Whithorn in the 1870's had made all this possible. You could catch the evening train from London and arrive in Newton Stewart next morning. Then across the platform to the local train for Wigtown, Kirkinner, Whauphill, Sorbie and Whithorn. And how to manage the last few miles? No problem since Reid's Posting Establishment advertised **"Bus meets 9.42 a.m. and 5.50 p.m. trains daily"**.

A SUMMER EVENING ISLE OF WHITHORN

This would have been a horse-drawn wagonette which took 40 minutes for the four miles from Whithorn station to the Isle. Having safely arrived, visitors could stay in the Steam Packet or Queen's Arms or take lodgings.   In the year 1900 the following were offered:

> **Mrs. Kyle – The Castle (6 apartments)**
> **A. McPhater – Dunbar House – 10 apartments**
> **Bath (hot and cold).   Piano.**
> **McWilliam Bros – Rosnat – 7 rooms;**
> **Seabreeze – 8 rooms; Willowbank – 7 rooms**
> **(All with "Gravitation Water")**

So what did the Isle have to offer then? Quite a lot, according to the guide:

"**A bowling green is open at nominal charge, and there are the conveniences of Church, Library and Postal Telegraph Office. The water supply is good, there being a gravitation supply besides a spa and other wells.**" There was also a nine-hole golf course "**very sporting, rich in hazards, has excellent drives**".   Perhaps 'hazards' entailed the risk of slicing your ball over the cliffs at Stein.

And of course there was the sea:

"**Reliable crafts in charge of reliable seamen can be hired, and fishing is attended with a gratifying amount of success.   There are many coves and nooks in which bathers may disport themselves in a clear transparent wave.**"

This reference to 'bathers' is nicely illustrated in this visitor's postcard from the Isle, written in August 1920:

"**This is a very quiet place, but there are some swanks, and mixed bathing. The weather has been too cold for me to shock them yet. The fishermen are novices compared with the East Coast. There is a bowling green and also two inns, so there is no fear of me wearying.**"

Reading the old Tours in Galloway guides it is surprising to find how little has changed here (pity about the golf).   The Isle is still that '**restorative for jaded nerves**' which the verbose writer of a hundred years ago described.

Let the Bard of Galloway have the last word:

> **How dear a spot is that between**
> **The points of Burrow Head and Stein,**
> **Where stands a sight for many a mile**
> **The hoary cairn which crowns 'the Isle'.**

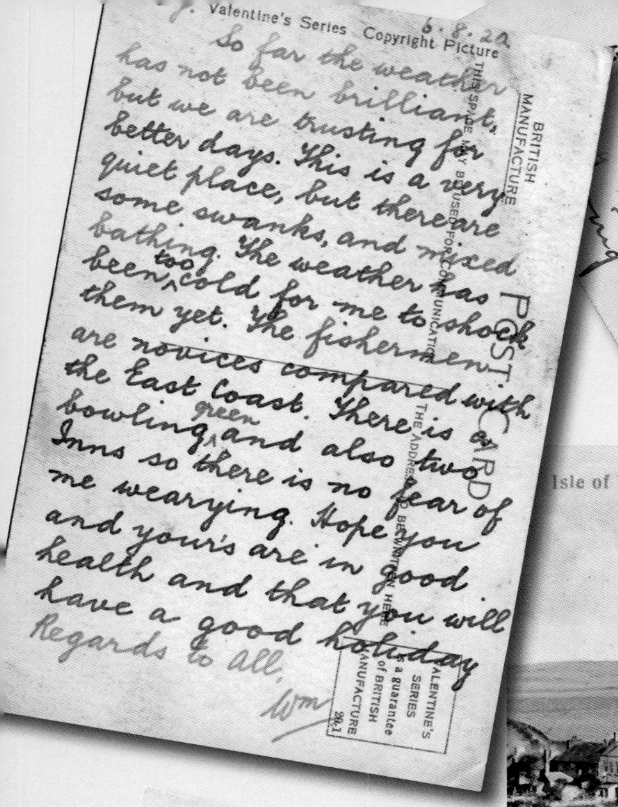

Valentine's Series Copyright Picture

BRITISH MANUFACTURE

So far the weather has not been brilliant, but we are trusting for better days. This is a very quiet place, but there are some swanks, and mixed bathing. The weather has been too cold for me to shock them yet. The fishermen are novices compared with the East coast. There is a bowling green, and also two Inns so there is no fear of me wearying. Hope you and your's are in good health and that you will have a good holiday. Regards to all,

Wm

POST CARD

THE ADDRESS TO BE WRITTEN HERE

VALENTINE'S SERIES

a guarantee of BRITISH MANUFACTURE

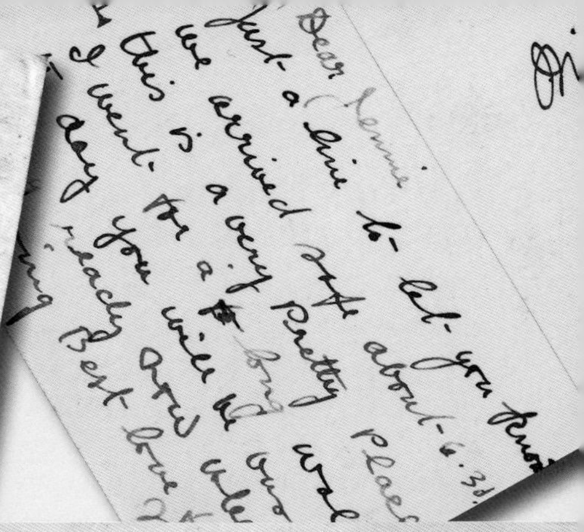

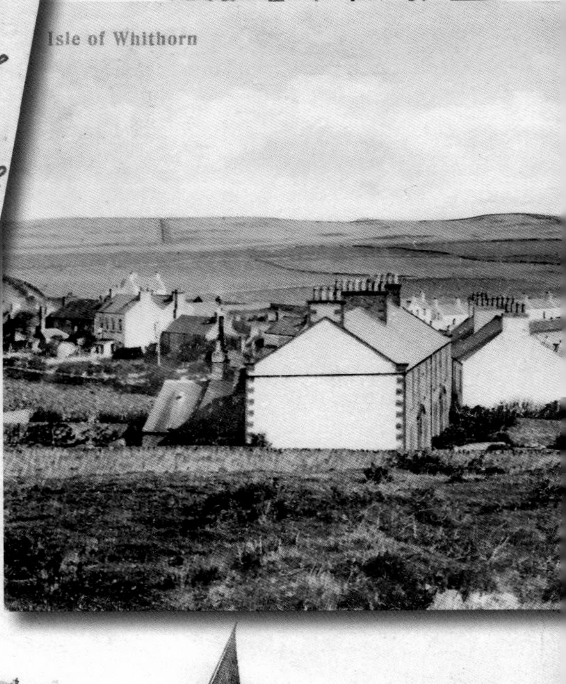

Dear Jennie,

Just a line to let you know we arrived safe about 6.30 this is a very pretty place. The a.f. is very big. I went, you will be our ready and we... Best love

Isle of Whithorn

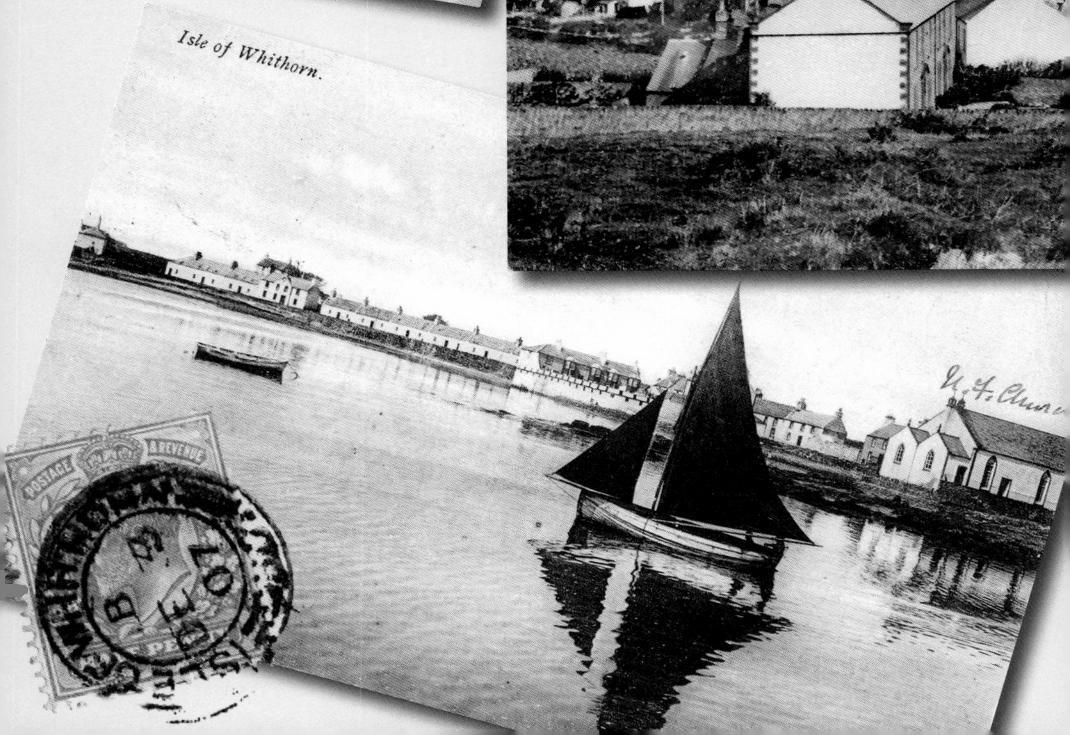

Isle of Whithorn.

5 - *Walk Back in Time*

John Scoular looks for links to our early history

The Machars peninsula has a plethora of important historical sites, many of them very early. Most are well known and easily identified by visitors and locals alike. A classical example is the site of the Iron Age fort on the Cairn at the Isle of Whithorn, where the ramparts and the early ridge and furrow cultivation are easily distinguished.

Also well known is Castle Feather, within the Burrowhead Camp site, though the Iron Age fort has been largely overwhelmed by later mediaeval additions. It is now probably best known to the modern generation as the setting for the imposing central figure in the cult film '*The Wicker Man*'.

Many of the sites in Galloway have not been examined in great detail – largely on economic grounds – so it is interesting to study the results of an important and recent excavation at a much less well known site – Carghidown, about a mile west of the Burrowhead Holiday Village.

This had a major investigation in both 2003 and 2004 by a team from the Glasgow University Archaeological Research Division. It is not easy to summarise its findings but it was an Iron Age promontory fort which had sporadic occupation over a period during the late first millennium BC or early first millennium AD.

It's been suggested that it was almost "shelter accommodation" - only resorted to when neighbourhood activity was particularly hostile. Whatever the reasons, the dig showed that the site was only formally enclosed during the latter stages of its occupation – and then its ramparts were violently thrown down and residence ceased.

Little now remains on the site after the dig's tidy up of its work and it is all too easy to pass it by, lying as it does in a very sheltered hollow at the cliff edge.

One of the more interesting finds at the site, however, were three lead beads which were of special importance to one of the dig team, Fraser Hunter, son of local historian Jack Hunter.

This brings us right up to date - a team from the Royal Commission on the Ancient and Historical Monuments of Scotland is currently

The impressive cliffs west of Burrowhead, looking along the shore of Luce Bay towards St. Ninian's Cave. Many historic sites lie close to the coastal path here.

Historic sites at
Carghidown
Mary Mine
Castle Feather

surveying and studying the area round the Mary Mine which lies about half a mile east of Carghidown.

Always known locally as the Copper Mine, it was also believed to have been associated with lead production. It is known to have been at least temporarily opened about the beginning of the First World War when mineral prices were high. But its main production period would probably be in the nineteenth century when the site was owned by the Stewart family of Physgill and Tonderghie.

One of the side issues of the present survey may be to show a link between the lead beads found at Carghidown and very early primitive mining and scratching of the surface. Like Carghidown, little remains to show the walker on the lovely cliff path from Burrowhead to St. Ninian's Cave – but it adds a touch of history to the natural beauty of the walk.

Mary Mine - one of the easily spotted areas that were still worked in the early 20th Century

On the set of *The Wicker Man* in 1973. The huge structure of the Wicker Man stands ready for the shooting of the final scene of the cult movie.

Photo by Byron Chamberlain

Blue squill flowers
carpet the clifftop walk
between St Ninian's
Cave and Burrowhead.

6 – *Walking the coastline*

John Scoular and Mike Marshall describe two dramatic walks around the Machars peninsula, from St. Ninian's Cave and Physgill Glen to Burrowhead and the Isle of Whithorn; and from the Isle of Whithorn via Cruggleton to Garlieston.

The network of paths around the Machars peninsula has been developing over the last few years, and the Isle of Whithorn is well placed as a hub from which to explore some spectacular and little known parts of our coastline.

None of the 28 km (17½ miles) of path is excessively arduous, but anybody undertaking the walks should take all reasonable precautions – especially with regard to footwear – flip-flops and sandals are inviting trouble, and vigorous undergrowth and thorn-laden shrubbery can leave painful evidence! The weather can and does change, and wind is always a feature of the more exposed stretches along the cliffs. Please take particular care here, and please respect the fact that the farmland you will be walking through may have a growing crop or grazing animals (with their young) on it. Keep dogs under strict control; take plenty of photographs, leave nothing but footprints!

St. Ninian's Cave and Physgill Glen to Burrowhead and the Isle

Spring in Physgill Glen - the path down to the beach passes through woods filled with the scent of wild garlic; a scene which has changed little, apart from the density of trees, since the post-card picture below was taken in 1904.

Unless you plan to walk in or out of Physgill Glen, you will need your own transport to get to Physgill Glen car park. From there, the path is well signed and takes you around the back of the Kidsdale farm buildings, crossing a local road and into the glen proper.

The track passes the beautiful Kidsdale farmhouse, reputedly a copy of a French chateau. The late Mrs. Nicholson of Kidsdale was a very fine gardener and this can be seen from glimpses of the garden when passing – and in the glen itself with some "fugitives" from the main gardens, including some fine specimens of gunnera.

The wood in the glen is completely self seeded after a post-war clear fell and boasts a host of woodland flowers and plants with magnificent bluebells, primroses, honeysuckle and wild garlic, together with true wild strawberries in season.

The view along the beach from St Ninian's Cave to Port Castle. The cave attracts many hundreds of people throughout the year, with an annual pilgrimage in August

Half way to the sea a track branches to the right with a 100 metre walk up to a very scenic waterfall.

Just below the junction is a very fine example of an estate crafted bridge over the stream.

Emerging onto the foreshore – a classic example of a storm beach – St. Ninian's Cave is immediately visible to the right at the end of the beach. The walk there veers along a beach noted for a tremendous variety of stone – granite, quartz. Few resist the chance for a paperweight but the beach doesn't seem to diminish – and it is a heavy carry home.

Returning from the cave along the beach, the coastal path zig-zags up the cliff, with Port Castle, the little fort guarding the entrance to the glen – one of many along the coast whose origins are uncertain.

At the top of the cliff path – proceed with care since it is a sunny sheltered corner much loved by adders. The flat rock faces on the right of the cliff bear the name of the deer, because they were once used as a target for militia and locals to fire at a painted red deer on the face. Ball marks can still be seen.

Keep a good lookout to sea for this is a popular fishing stretch for seals and even otters.

Bird life on the cliffs includes the usual sea birds, but ravens and peregrines are also likely to be seen. The path follows the cliff edge very closely around here, and there are some spectacular views into the deep clefts of shattered rocks.

At Carghidown there is evidence of recent archaeological work on the old forts, (see previous chapter), a true history of which is still under review but the site is remarkable in that it is almost completely concealed from landward until almost under foot.

Half a mile further on the shafts of the Mary Mine can be seen on the foreshore. Known locally as the Copper Mine it was certainly mined for lead up to the period of the First World War – at least one of the miners, originally from Wales, being buried in Whithorn churchyard. Research is at present going on to link possible early scratchings at the vein – part of which can be seen running out seaward in a gulley – with early metalwork found at Carghidown.

Continuing east and keeping a careful eye on the very varied cliff top flora with a lot of unusual plants, you reach Burrowhead and the Holiday Village. The original camp was built in the pre-war period as a training base for anti-aircraft gunners. Traces of an earlier war background can be seen in the wall of Castle Feather, another of the cliff top forts.

But the headland is now chiefly famous as the dramatic setting for the film *"The Wicker Man"* - a burning of a giant effigy on the cliff edge, and which formed a spectacular sunset setting for the fire sequence.

St Ninian's Cave can be seen in the distance; the only steep climb on this route is up from the beach at Port Castle to begin the coastal walk. Keep a careful watch for adders which like to bask in the sunshine

There are some spectacular cliffscapes to be seen along the coastal paths. This view is taken just north of Burrowhead, with the ex-World War II gunnery observation post still present

Treasure hunters have long since removed the remains of the monster legs of the Wicker Man which stood for years before the film attained cult status.

After leaving the camp area Burrowhead itself is reached and soon after the remains of a concrete building from which observers could safely watch the attempts of the gunners to shoot down, in the early days of the Second World War, a radio-controlled Queen Bee target seaplane or latterly a drone towed by aircraft stationed at West Freugh.

The last military use of the camp was as a holding post for Polish soldiers while the British Government tried to make up their mind what to do about them after the end of the war. Quite a few stayed behind and made their own lives in Scotland.

Just east of Burrowhead a spit of rock runs out culminating in a solitary pinnacle known as the Old Man. On this spit there is also a perfect natural arch, known as the Devil's Bridge, with inshore a flat platform of rock on which there are many "footprints" – also known, inevitably, as the devil's footprints.

Just beyond the spit is the Jimmy Hole, a very useful little cave with a landing beach once popular with smugglers. Also painted on the rock face there, but now no longer visible, was a white slab painted and known as the Manxman's compass, as it gave a true north bearing from the Isle of Man.

A spring shower passes over Wigtown Bay - the Kirkcudbright coast just visible in the distance

The clifftop path now meanders downhill and again you should keep a keen lookout for both sea birds and seals.   They are particularly abundant when you come to the reefs guarding the entrance to the bay at Isle of Whithorn.   Known as "The Screens" they are in a particularly nasty stretch of strong flowing tidal water which makes it difficult for sailors – ancient and modern – to judge safe entry into the bay.   More than one vessel met its end on the screens – or knocked down the navigation "perch" which used to provide a marker for the end of the reef.

The path now descends quietly back to the village past a series of little coves which were for years the happy hunting ground for generations of picnickers, young and old, - and are still popular today.

The remarkable outline
of the arch at Cruggleton
Castle is visible for almost
all of the coastal walk north
from the Isle

The Isle to Garlieston

Unlike the often vertiginous path that goes from the Isle to Burrowhead and St Ninian's Cave, this section isn't as demanding – but the views and the peace of the countryside that borders this part of Wigtown Bay are just as delightful.

A really attractive feature is that it is 'do-able' on a one-way basis in conjunction with the local bus service. Walk the path to Garlieston, and catch the bus back to the Isle in time for well-deserved refreshment, or more. Walking in a northerly direction also means that you (usually) have the wind to your back, and in good weather, the sun is behind you.

Allow a good three hours for your yomp to Garlieston – allow a bit more if you want to take a longer picnic break along the way. The going is easy, no stiff climbs, and you follow the shoreline for the most part. There are very few areas where you are exposed to sheer cliffs. Where these do occur, mainly around Cruggleton, the path is kept to the landward side of long-established dykes and fences. A couple of bridges have been built to negotiate substantial burns.

There are two options for starting this walk. The first, and not the easiest at present, is to start at the Laigh Isle chalets, and follow a well-used meandering path up the cliff to Stein Head. There are some lovely, different views of the Isle from this side of the village, and at the summit there's an Ordnance Survey triangulation pillar with a superb view over to Wigtown Bay.

Looking south to the Isle from Cruggleton Point

The Isle of Whithorn,
seen from the north
near Stein Head

From here it is possible to make a descent following the coast around Cairnhead to the shore at Portyerrock. But as this section has only recently been added to the path network there are as yet (May 2010) no waymarking or kissing gates to avoid the occasional up-and-over at dykes. If speed is a priority it might be better to walk from the Isle up the B7004 road towards Portyerrock – passing Stannock road end, Isle Farm and Cairnhead. Portyerrock has very limited lay-by space for parking a car, so be warned.

At Portyerrock there is a well-signed kissing gate, where the trail takes you down past Portyerrock Mill to the shore, and almost immediately you have the world to yourself. Oystercatchers, unaccustomed to seeing much human presence shriek out their alarm calls and provide dazzling flights of black and white plumage. Opposite Sheddock, and barely ten minutes from the start, a peaceful little bay – the Howe Hole – invites an immediate pause for contemplative refreshment! There are usually some sociable horses who might enjoy your visit too!

And then on up the coast – although the path isn't particularly evident, the waymarking posts are helpful, and the kissing gates at field boundaries are easily spotted.

Up past Dinnans, and then on towards Palmallet and you're in prime stock-rearing country – inquisitive suckler cows with their calves, and a change of scene as sure-footed sheep glance up from their grazings to watch your gentle progress upwards with the lie of the land.

Look out for old and new fortifications along the way – at Dinnans, old earth ramparts, possibly Iron Age, can be seen surrounding a more recent concrete look-out post – a reminder of the strategic role of this part of the coastline in the development of the Mulberry harbours in the Second World War.

All the time on this walk towards Cruggleton Point the Castle with its much-decayed arch looms ever closer. Plenty of scope for photographs here with this dramatic cliffscape constantly changing appearance. Be especially wary of the sheer cliffs at the Castle.

From here the path descends towards Rigg Bay and Garlieston, and at the entrance into Cruggleton Woods, past a lodge house that has been recently renovated.

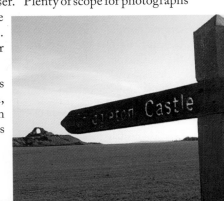

The path winds through a delightful 'magic' tangle of oak, beech and ash trees, and during spring there's an equally magic carpet of wild garlic, bluebells, primroses and campion.

The sheltered beach at Rigg Bay

As you get closer to Garlieston a small diversion into Galloway House Gardens more than repays your time spent on foot, especially in springtime – there are plenty of places to sit, relax, enjoy the birdsong and reflect on your journey along one of our least-known stretches of coastline.

Galloway House Gardens in springtime

The coastal path proceeds out through Garlieston to the north, still following the shore, and ends at present at Innerwell, where there is access to a public road and limited car parking. In time, it's hoped that access agreements will enable the completion of the Machars Coastal Path right around the peninsula, and link into a wider network of routes across south-west Scotland. You will find the Ordnance Survey Explorer series map No. 311 indispensable.

7 – *The Isle in Wartime*
by John Scoular

The postcard above shows the basic accommodation that was on hand for the service personnel posted there for anti-aircraft training. Pleasant enough perhaps on fine days, but when there's a storm blowing...

Local labour was brought in to help build the camp headquarters.

The army camp at Burrowhead was built rather hurriedly just before the Second World War as a training camp for anti-aircraft gunners while the country was in the process of re-arming. The idea was that an aircraft would fly up and down in front of the guns, which would try to bring it down. Initially, radio-controlled 'Queen Bee' aircraft were used, and the flat concrete foundation by the white tower on the Cairn was laid down for one of the control huts. Here one of the pilots involved could "fly" the target aircraft down the range. This was a float-equipped Tiger Moth which was catapulted from Burrowhead and

landed on the sea after the practice firing to be taken back to the little RAF station at Kidsdale, where it would be prepared for the next mission. It was uneconomic to keep using the 'Queen Bee', so obsolete aircraft were brought in to West Freugh to be towed as drones in front of the guns - the idea being that the gunners shot at the drones and not the aircraft! A fleet of small craft was based in the Isle to service the operation - several patrol vessels and one that was responsible for lifting the downed drone and taking it back for refurbishment. The concrete plinth remains by the white tower, and is now home to the poignant memorial to the crew of the *Solway Harvester*.

The A-A gun emplacements, and below, a view of the Isle harbour with an RAF patrol vessel under way

A slipway down to the water was built in front of the old lifeboat house to bring up the RAF patrol boats when bad weather was forecast, particularly strong south-easterly winds.

THE BAY. ISLE OF WHITHORN.

The RAF had their own weather station which was supposed to forecast bad weather, and on two separate occasions the Head Coastguard, John Maguire, warned them that bad weather was approaching, but the warning was disregarded - with the result that they lost two craft.

The local ladies ran a very popular WVS (Women's Voluntary Service) canteen at the end of the harbour for the hundreds of troops who were here.

Troops at Burnside in the Isle

In the latter war years the village's major contribution was undoubtedly the preparations for the Normandy invasion – the new, legendary, Mulberry Harbour. At the time few locals realized the importance of what was going on.   True, access on the Garlieston road was restricted to those living there and the bay at Portyerrock was filled with strange ships and constructions.   But it was much later before it was realised how important the area had been as a test bed for the coming invasion.

W/762... Hut 5. 472 ...
H.A.A. Practice Camp,
Whithorn,
Wigtownshire,
Scotland.

Monday.

My Dear Mother

Well. I'm still here, alive & kicking. Or rather slithering. Gosh! the mud in this place. Everywhere we go, its mud, mud, mud! Oh, & before I forget, has Dad any old socks? These boots are miles too big. I wear another ...

Troops march up Tondergie Row to Burrowhead. They would have probably come by train to Whithorn station, four miles away

Little remains as evidence of the activity. A couple of brick buildings where the engineers' camp once stood, and in one little inlet the remains of a concrete pontoon, left by the military as a thank-you to the Head Coastguard. It provided a little harbour for the small boat he used in connection with the now defunct Portyerrock salmon fishery.

There are one or two villagers who can remember the wartime days when, returning home from school, they would observe servicemen making their way from the canteen on the harbour back to Burrowhead camp: "The soldiers always seemed to be marching back to camp as we came out of school so we "marched" along behind them singing *We had a good job for thirty bob, with a left, right, left.* It was a good way to get home more quickly, though it was a struggle to keep up, especially going up Rosie's Brae."

8 – The Isle and the Land

Away from the sea, the village is surrounded by good farmland and those who lived and worked on this land have played a considerable part in village life.   As with any occupation, there have been many changes over the years, and often the impact on our community and its way of life was notable.   Dorothy McIlwraith, David Brown and Wilma Brown compiled this major article for the Isle's website in 2002, and it is presented here with subsequent revisions.

The Farms

There are four farms immediately surrounding the village, Cutreoch, Boyach, Stannock and Isle Farm. From the farm names, it would appear that the settlements date from early times. Isle Farm was obviously named after the village; Cutreoch may well come from a mix of Britonic/ Gaelic and means "cold cottage".

Boyach (originally Buyoch - "yellow field") named possibly because of the yellow whins (gorse) that grow around the farm. Stannock possibly meant "stone house", but interestingly was previously known as Stennock Corbett and was part of Stennock Balconnell. (It's not certain if the ruins at the back of the farm were originally a separate holding).

Boyach farmhouse about 1900

The ownership of farms is interesting too. Most of the farms in the Machars belonged to the church in the 16th Century. Boyach and Cutreoch, along with Morrach and Tonderghie belonged to Dundrennan Abbey, while Stannock, Prestrie, Arbrack, Sheddock and Cutcloy belonged to Whithorn Priory. In time they were sold to successive large, wealthy landowners such as the Stewarts, Houstons, Vaus and Stairs.

In 1878, it appears that Isle Farm, along with Bysbie and the Mill, were on the Physgill estate of the Earl of Galloway. Stannock and Falhar (see later) had been bought by the Earl of Stair from the Earl of Galloway in 1874. Cutreoch was on the Castlewigg estate and Boyach on the Tonderghie estate.

Stannock old farmhouse

From Slater's directory of 1893, the farmers were noted as
Cutreoch - John G Martin;
Boyach - Alexander Donnan (along with High Ersock);
Stannock: Ivie McIlwraith;
Falhar - Jane Douglas;
Isle Farm - William B Waugh,
and also Isle Farm - Agnes & Alex. Fraser.

We can only assume that one of the names farmed at Isle Farm as we now know it, and the other at Isle Croft (the sheds just outside the village on the west side of the Garlieston road) which is now a part of Isle Farm.

Falhar has disappeared. In 1946 it was sold by Stannock to Lindsay of Low Mains. After the house burned down in 1950's it was bought by the Vances of Portyerrock and amalgamated into that farm.

Cutreoch was farmed by Bill Brown (who also owned Morrach), then Miss Clark and, for a short time, Jim Young, before being sold to Robin Simpson, the present occupant.

Cutreoch Farm in the 1920's

Mrs Palmer was in Boyach and then from 1938, Sidney Cummings, before being taken over by Eben Brown (of Drummoral) in 1943, the present farmer being his grandson, David. Stannock was farmed by the McIlwraith family until 2006 when it was sold to the Cathers family from Northern Ireland.

Isle Farm is currently farmed by Tom Forsyth who bought it from Hugh Watson around 1970, having been previously owned by Bobby Cummings.

Isle Farm probably around 1910

The land within the village mainly belonged to James Alexander, the miller at Bysbie Mill, and who lived in what is now the Post Office. His farm buildings were on the site on which a new house (aptly named Millers Byre) now stands. He had a boat shed and slipway at Donegal - the Miller's Port, and the pigsties opposite his house were next to the Drummullin Burn, allowing him to feed live eels to his pigs - a treat they seemed to thoroughly enjoy.

The farm buildings where Miller's Byre now stands

Everywhere can be seen "dry-stane dykes" - walls built of stones which surround much of our farm land.   There have always been many excellent local craftsmen - fortunately it is a trade that is still attracting young men.

Below - a prizewinning Ayrshire herd at Stannock Farm in the 1950's.

The People who worked on the Land

Today, most of the farms are worked by the farmer and his family with some hired help, much of it in the form of contractors who deal with operations such as harvesting, silage making, spreading fertiliser, crop spraying, and slurry spreading. The contractors often come from some distance away with large machinery and supply their own labour.

In days past however things were different. Then, all the work with the exception perhaps of the visit of the threshing mill, was undertaken by the farm staff and locally sourced casual labour. Farming was much more labour intensive in these days, and the farms were small communities in themselves where whole families worked, some full-time and some casually at the busier periods. Up to the 1950's most of the farms had 6-8 regular employees, and with two cottages on Cutreoch; one (in earlier times) on Boyach; three on Stannock, and two on Isle Farm, most of these workers lived in the village. In those times every farm had, depending on their stock and crops, a dairyman, milkers, stockmen, horsemen, tractormen (when tractors became popular), a pigman, and although they would all help with general farm tasks, they each dealt with their own specialisation.

Present-day farming is a much lonelier job, a very different occupation in many ways. Multi-skilling is essential - a general farm worker must be able not only to feed and work with stock, but drive a tractor, and often a forklift or small digger. He (or she) must be able to treat the stock when ill, maintain and repair machinery, and ensure that the ever increasing number of rules and regulations are complied with – all of which add to the stress of the job.

Another noticeable change has been within the womenfolk on the farms. In the early years women made up a considerable percentage of farm labour, many hand milking twice daily, hoeing and shawing turnips, helping with haymaking, harvesting and mill days and maybe even working horses.

The farmhouse was a busy place, with many mouths to feed, never mind the cleaning and washing. It was very common for a farmhouse to have a live-in maid and often extra daily help.

In many families one daughter remained unmarried to help with the chores and look after her parents as they became older. What a change a century has wrought!

Now most farmers' daughters head for university or college and high-powered jobs. Even if they do return and marry their "handsome farmer", most continue to work, and although lending what help and support they can, life in the farmhouse is definitely different.

The pattern of meals and the food on the table has also changed considerably. Even in 1960's a dairy farmer's day would

Waiting for the snow plough to pass in 1960 - milk is being taken to Whithorn creamery.

commence with tea and home-made cake at 5.30 am. When milking was done, there was a breakfast of porridge, bacon and egg, and toast. A mid-morning cuppa came with a fresh scone and then, at noon, there was home-made soup, meat and two veg. and a baked or steamed pudding.

Work would go on until 4 pm when there would be a tea - a selection of scones with cheese and home-made jam and a variety of cakes and buns, freshly baked of course. After evening milking, perhaps poached egg or fish would be enjoyed and then, to round off the day, tea and sandwiches at bedtime. A far cry from today's cereal breakfast, soup at lunchtime, hastily grabbed chocolate biscuits and crisps and a good substantial main meal at night - and often only one course! It might seem a healthier diet but are today's farmers healthier? Is their health dictated by the food they eat or the more stressful and solitary lifestyle they lead?

The Stock

Like all other farms in this area in the early part of last century, Cutreoch, Boyach, Stannock and Isle Farm all had herds of brown and white Ayrshire milking cows. Then, all the cows had horns. Today these are removed when the animals are very young as they serve no useful purpose and would only cause injury to others in herd or the stockmen. Today only Stannock and Isle Farm have milking herds, each having large herds of black & white Holsteins.

These cattle are bred to provide a large quantity of good quality milk (averaging roughly 14,000 pints per cow per year) and are milked single-handed in modern computerised milking parlours.

Cutreoch and Boyach farms now concentrate on beef production. Boyach has about 140 Aberdeen-Angus cross-suckler cows and followers mated with a Limousin bull. At Cutreoch and Morrach cattle are fattened inside during the winter, and both inside and outside in the summer, and there is also a small herd of distinctive Belted Galloways.

Belted Galloway cattle.

All the farms have at one time or another had pigs, but never on a large scale, with the exception of Cutreoch, which kept 200 pigs during the Second World War and fed them on the swill from Burrowhead Army camp. An eagle eye had to be kept for "foreign bodies" such as cutlery and razor blades! All the farms also kept hens, often just for their own use. Cutreoch had 1000 White Leghorns, and every egg had to be wiped clean and all cracked ones removed before packing them into 30-dozen egg boxes. All this for 9 old pence (just under 4p) rising to 11½ d (just under 5p) around 1946!

Early in the twentieth century, Clydesdale horses provided much of the power on all the farms, and the visit of the stallion was a notable event as, under his groom, he moved from farm to farm, both horse and master being welcome guests. Horses would be walked to the smiddy to be shod, some at Glasserton by John or Leslie Hawkins, while others went to Tommy & Hughie Woods at Sorbie. Although there are still a number of Clydesdales in the southern Machars there are none immediately around the village.

In the early 1900's cattle droves took place from the farms to Whithorn railway station for loading onto cattle wagons to go to market. If the cattle had to stay overnight in Whithorn the gates were put up at the Portmouth (the narrow part of the road at the south end of the town), and what is now the Essentials shop, and so they were corralled in George Street.

Tommy Woods

The Crops

At one time farms were fairly self sufficient in feeding and bedding for their stock and to this end every farm grew corn (mainly oats), made hay, and grew turnips and sugar beet for winter feed.

Boyach, Isle Farm and Cutreoch also grew early potatoes that were sold to merchants in Glasgow and Edinburgh, and usually went by rail from Whithorn station. "Gaffers" from the west of Ireland brought their squads of "tattie howkers" over every year to the same farms to lift the early potatoes. Late potatoes were a smaller crop in this area, so the school children had time off in October to lift them - remembered by the fact that the school October holiday was for many years nicknamed the "Tattie" holiday.

Cutreoch also grew carrots. When Sydney Cummings farmed Boyach during the war vegetables were grown and sold mainly to Burrowhead Army camp. All these crops were very labour intensive and weather dependent.

Silage-making at Isle Farm in 2008

As time has passed the main crop grown for animal feed is silage - grass, which is finely chopped and placed in pits or packed and wrapped as sealed plastic bales where it ferments and produces an easily worked and highly palatable feed.

In the early days of silage-making each layer of grass was sprayed with a solution of treacle and water before being rolled to compress it. The cattle loved the extra sweetness, the farm kids loved licking the treacle barrel, and the molasses made the best ever gingerbreads!

Some cereal crops such as barley and maize, seen here, are now grown at Stannock and Isle Farm, and also made into an arable silage.

The Mills, Buyers and Suppliers

Back in medieval times, mills were associated with religious houses, burghs or estates and their function was to process grain from tenants and estate owners. The late 17th and 18th Centuries saw growth in the number of mills to meet the demand of markets in England. After 1850 there was a gradual decline as arable farming gave way to dairying. Small mills closed as larger mills developed at Stranraer, Dalbeattie and Dumfries. Locally the only mills in operation in recent times were at Port William and Garlieston.

There are frequent records through the centuries of Bysbie Mill in the Isle. It was connected to the lands of the Barony of Busby and all the corn grown on the lands was required to be put through the Barony's mill and taxes had to be paid by the tenants. Eventually Bysbie came under the title of Tonderghie lands, but as the mill's Charter had been lost the revenue could not be claimed. The last miller, James Alexander (grandfather of John Scoular), sold the mill in the 1930's to James Wyllie. Until 1945 Bysbie Mill (located behind the Queens Arms), with its miller Hughie Maxwell, would grind the grain from the local farms. When this ended it was used for grain storage with the wheel being removed, the dam breached and water channel filled in for safety reasons. The building itself is now in a sad condition and there is some doubt as to ownership. The millstones lie at the back of the Steam Packet Hotel.

Bysbie Mill at the Isle

A look at the deeds of the Old Mill at Portyerrock shows it was part of Portyerrock Farm owned by the Earl of Stair up until 1920, when it was sold to farmer John Black. A map dated 1826 shows 'Port Yarrock' farm and 'Port Yarrock Mill'. In 1953, it was converted into a house. It's been difficult to establish when the mill last operated, and although part of the water channel to the lade is still visible, the water wheel is long gone and no machinery or grinding stones exist.

Portyerrock Mill

Right up to the 1970's there was a feed depot in Whithorn where farmers could get weedkillers, detergents and general supplies, and also an agricultural machinery depot, a blacksmith and a vet. Today, just the vet remains, with the other services located further and further away. At one time the sea was the main method of transport with coal and fertiliser arriving by boat. The advent of the railway to Whithorn brought more change - coal and fertiliser being collected at the station, and produce such as eggs, cheese and wool being dispatched in the same way. With all the local mills closed, feed now comes in bulk by road from Cumbria, Aberdeenshire and even further afield.

At one time Stannock made cheese but otherwise all the milk went to the creamery in Whithorn. That closed in 1974 and the new creamery built at Sorbie closed in 1992. Bladnoch creamery closed soon after. These were repeated blows not only to the farms but to several village families who were employed in them. The nearest factory for our milk is now in Stranraer, but sometimes it travels much further afield than that.

Our nearest livestock market is still in Newton Stewart, but most of the cattle and sheep from this area are sold privately or by deadweight, and are transported by road to Central Scotland or Northern England.

A short break during the harvest at Boyach in 1966

A Farmer's Diary

Compare a 1950's farmer's diary with today and we can certainly see big differences.

In times past, the first months of the year were spent doing the cold, back-breaking work of hand-shawing (cutting off the stalks) of turnips. These would feed the animals along with hay, which was usually forked in or broken out of small bales.

Nowadays, the main feed is silage, either from a pit or big bales, and distributed by a modern, heated tractor and loader.

Ploughing in 1978

This same machine deals with big bales of hay and straw that are also fed. The silage itself used to be hand-graped (forked) out, but now all the farms have feeder wagons, which can mix and chop rations and come with computerised weighing facilities so that a complex diet (especially for the dairy cattle) can be prepared and distributed.

The fields to be cropped or reseeded still have to be ploughed but now a big tractor and often a reversible 3- or 4-furrow plough has replaced the old horse and single furrow implement.

But whatever the method, the stones turned up by the plough still have to be lifted by hand. It's a tiring job and, in these days of small labour forces, often the farm families have to be cajoled into action. (This is one of the few jobs where children can still help as, with big machines and few people around, farms can be dangerous places - they are certainly not playgrounds).

Seventy years ago, May was a busy month on the farms when the corn was sown (prior to the mid 1940's this was done with a sowing sheet or a "fiddle"). The turnips were also sown by the third week in May, and two or three weeks later they were ready for hoeing.

Now, May and June brings the first cut of silage, and even this operation has progressed from the early days when a small chopper or forage wagon took at least a week to ten days to complete the job - sometimes much longer if the weather was not on your side. Now, it is made with a self-propelled chopper and transported in large trailers, so 80 to 100 acres can be cleared in a day.

Haymaking in the 1930's...

Hay is still made, but not nearly as much. The old way was to cut the grass with a reaper; it was then turned by hand forks and made into rucks (small stacks) by sweeping four rows of hay into bundles. The rucks were then hoisted by a rucklifter onto a cart, taken to the stackyard where stacks were built, and thatched with straw.

...and in the 1960's

Now hay is made by cutting with a disc mower, machine turning and baling. One similarity remains however - you still need good weather to make good hay! Wet days in the summer are still a time for tidying up but, where weeds used to be hand-cut by scythes, now there are machines for that job too.

Harvesting oats with a binder and stooking in the 1960's

Harvest was the next major task. Today, combine harvesters and the ability to dry the barley, or even store it while damp following treatment with propionic acid, make that task much quicker and less weather dependent. Compare that to the old way, when the corn was cut by scythes; reapers followed, and in the '30's - binders. A team of people lifted the straw into bundles, called sheaves (unless there was a binder that did it for you!), and

built six or eight of them into a stook. These were left for about two weeks of good weather before they were carted in. If the weather wasn't too kind it would be necessary to turn or shift the stooks – 'stook hunting' was not a popular job!

Building the stacks of corn was a job that needed many pairs of hands -

Harvest teas were always eagerly awaited!

When the stooks had been brought to the yard, they were built into stacks by an experienced builder, aided by a handler (often known as a hanger!). In poor weather the harvest could take several months, and so almost ran into the period when the mill came round to thresh the corn to provide some of the winter feed.

The steam traction engine came from Whithorn for the Mill Days

Mill Days, as they were known, were special. The mill would arrive the night before threshing began, and it towed a wooden sleeping hut, where the two mill men would spend the night. Early the next morning they lit the fire to get steam up and came up to the farmhouse for their breakfast. It was a fairly labour intensive operation, so sometimes farms joined up and pooled their workers.

One man forked sheaves from the stack onto the mill where two (normally women - described as "handers") cut the strings and handed them to the millman who fed them into the mill. The oats came out at four different chutes depending on their quality - two chutes of good stock feed, one for hen feed, and the last with the rubbish! It took two men to deal with the oats, seeing the bags were properly filled, changing them, tying up and moving the full ones.

At the other end of the threshing machine the straw came out in "bunches" - these were forked by yet another busy pair of hands to the stack builder. From the side of the mill came "chaff" onto a large sheet made from two opened hessian sacks. This was carried away to provide bedding for the cattle. The farmhouse was also a busy place on mill days. Not only did the mill men require all their meals, but everyone looked forward to the big pots of soup, and all kinds of home-made scones and cakes.

The mill came usually once a month through the winter. After the war paraffin fuelled tractors (later, diesel), replaced the steam traction engine. With the advent of combine harvesters in the late 1950's mill days became a thing of the past - not missed for the hard work they entailed, but for the fun and friendships lost.

Harvesting today - speedy, and lonely

The wool harvest at Drummoral in 1965

Sheep Clipping

The farm staff did this by hand. Again, this was a labour-intensive occupation, men gathering the sheep and taking away those that had been clipped. The sheep were caught and passed to the shearers. They originally worked with hand shears until engine-powered mechanical shears (similar to those still used), were introduced. The fleece was handed to another man who rolled it up and tied it with some of the belly wool that had been made into a rope. This was thirsty work, and the staple drink was "oatmeal water" - a couple of handfuls of oatmeal in a can of water. The wool was piled in rolls and taken to the loft for the next process (a wet day job) when it was packed into special hessian bags or sheets provided by the Wool Board. Often somebody would go right inside the bag to pack it and tramp it in properly. These bags then went by train from Whithorn station to the Wool Board in Paisley.

Things have not changed too drastically as sheep still have to be sheared, but now this is mainly done by teams of shearers with mobile clipping units. Shearing was always a busy day in the farmhouse kitchen, although today it's more often pizzas or fish & chips followed by chocolate biscuits, and all washed down with cans of fizzy drinks.

Show Days

The Wigtown Show was the biggest day of the year for most farm workers when they could go and meet friends and family from other farms - for many it was perhaps the only meeting in the year. Today, the show still attracts a large crowd and retains its happy atmosphere. Showing pedigree stock has not changed much over the years – the conformation of the "ideal" animal may be somewhat different but the work and skill required has changed little. Preparing stock for showing is a lengthy business. The animals have to be picked out many months, even years, in advance and watched carefully to see if they have "potential".

As the show comes nearer, they have to be worked with frequently so that they will be easy to handle amidst the crowds and noise. Just like anyone going out to impress, they need to have their hair trimmed, washed and set, hopefully to catch the judge's eye. Some animals really seem to enjoy this while others are just not suitable for showing.

Local shows are good fun, if hard work. It is often a 3 am start to get the rest of the stock dealt with before the show animals leave.

A Stannock Ayrshire cow ready for the ring at the Wigtown Show in 1968

It's important to get them into the show field early so they have time to settle and to sort any areas that have got dirty on the journey. The men also take an opportunity to grab something to eat (thus the boxes and baskets of rolls and flasks beside each farm's entries), probably not having had time for breakfast and anticipating a long wait before they can relax again when the showing is over. Rarely is there time for even a walk round the show field before it is time to set off for home to take up the day-to-day chores. However, the people you meet make up for all the worries, and there is the opportunity to show off stock to potential customers!

For National events such as the Royal Highland Show at Edinburgh it's necessary to take the animals one or two days ahead of the show, and keep them there for the four-day duration of the event. This requires making sure that all the usual day-to-day activities at home are still dealt with. It is, nevertheless, a wonderful experience, mixing with fellow breeders from all over the country. Bringing home silverware from there is something you don't readily forget.

A Stannock Holstein is Wigtown Show Champion 2003

9 - A Pleasant Place to do Business...

One major project undertaken by *Isle News* during its nine years of publication was to attempt to present a definitive description of the many businesses that existed at one time or another in the Isle.

Billy Brown and John Scoular undertook the lengthy researches - whether they were shops, or basic industries like carpenters and shoemakers. . .

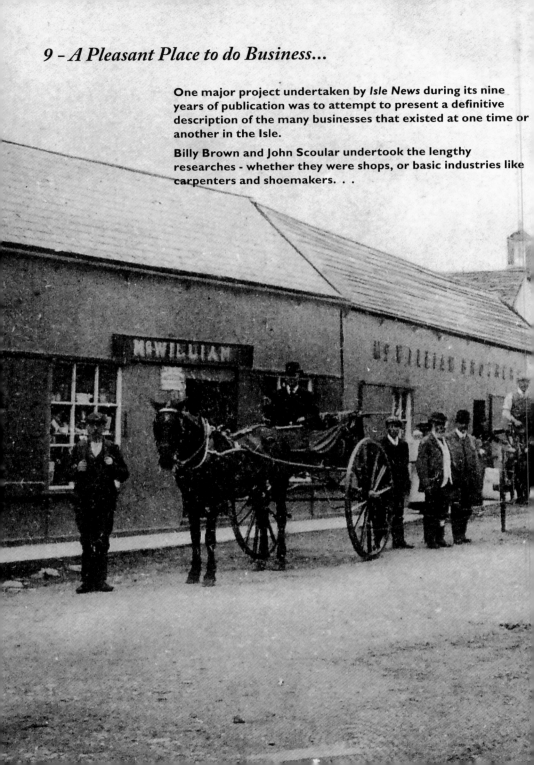

It is difficult to go back accurately before the beginning of the 1800's but that ever useful guide, Pigot's Directory of Wigtownshire, gives some clues as to the village's diverse employment when it was published in 1837. Some of the names listed are familiar even today. The directory describes Isle of Whithorn as *"a pleasant village, about three miles from Whithorn, of which it is the port. The coastguard has an establishment here under the command of a lieutenant of the Royal Navy."*

But the list of business people is formidable – there was a blacksmith, three boot and shoemakers, and no less than ten grocers and tea dealers were listed. There were five innkeepers and vintners, two joiners and wrights and two tailors. Finally, there was a miller, a ship's carpenter and an intriguingly titled 'tidewaiter' (a customs officer).

Although where and when all these businesses were carried on is not recorded, but many of the names survive at least in the pedigrees of some of the older Isle families.

A busy place the village was then and now, even if present occupations differ. Today it's perhaps more relevant to list some of the businesses and their characterful owners – which the writers can remember – or about whom they were told as youngsters.

An early 1900's view of Donaldson's shop

It's easiest to begin working down the village from opposite the Bowling Green. First to be recalled, and a happy memory for many of the older villagers, was Donaldson's shop. One remembers the tinkle of the bell as one stepped down into the shop and the always warm and smiling presence of Mrs. Donaldson ready to supply all manner of groceries – and sweets the like of which are not seen today and which could keep one sucking away for ages. Husband Bob was a bit of a character and drove a van, which pre-Second World War, was an invaluable link to the rural areas, farmers and cot-folk alike. This was an era when it was just not possible to pop down to the village shop.

Bob – (his favourite phrase *"I trust in God. All others cash"*) and his wife brought up a family all of whom – Louis, Doreen and Margaret – made their own mark on the Galloway community far beyond the Isle.

Virtually next-door was a business under a name still well known in the village today. Andrew Huxtable was the cobbler and shoemaker.

One of the biggest problems for anyone tracing the business history of the Isle is to follow the progress of the Post Office from place to place. Amateur archaeologists can have quite a time looking at house walls to determine which ones at various periods had held the all-important letter box. There are quite a few.

The writer's first recollection was of the service being run by the Curran family, just up the lane from the Queen's Arms. This was also a shoe shop and library. Postal services then went to McWilliam's shop with Mrs. McEwan as postmistress, before coming back up the road to Ambrose's shop, then the Ambrose house in Tonderghie Row. It then moved to the Cronie family home at Marville, then back up the hill to the Café before returning to its present home with Margaret Cronie – who also runs the sole surviving general store.

Across the lane from the Queens Arms

The Ambrose family previously mentioned had in fact initially taken over and moved across the road from where Alex Trew and his sister ran a very comprehensive grocery business - plus another of the vans, which served the rural area – before they moved away from the district.

Continuing down the road we come to the Queen's Arms, surely one of the Machars' most historic howffs. It has seen many licensees over the years going back within living memory to the Reid family. Jane Reid was a formidable lady who kept the till contents in the apron round her waist. And what was her box bed can still be seen on the right in the entrance hall. The Customs and Excise had their premises on the corner opposite and the Reids – possibly with

A 1935 view of Main Street with the Queens Arms on the left

some justification – used to keep a careful eye on their doings, suspecting that some of their seized contraband came in for personal consumption, doing the Queen's out of trade.

Directly opposite the Queen's was the Café, built just previous to the Second World War and run as a business until it was quite recently turned into a private house.   It was built originally to cash in on the trade that the newly established artillery training camp at Burrowhead brought to the village The camp had a huge influence on village life because thousands of service people trained there over the war years.   Although a bus service ran from the camp to the sophisticated fleshpots of Whithorn – particularly the cinema – the Isle businesses still benefited dramatically.   The local ladies for many years under the auspices of the Womens' Voluntary Service ran a canteen in the harbour premises of James Wyllie which was much appreciated by all local serving military men and women.   It was situated past the 'Smugglers' building at the end of the Harbour.

Down the lane beside the Queen's Arms was the Bysbie Mill, where grain from local farms was processed. James Alexander, John Scoular's grandfather, owner of the mill in the thirties lived in what is now Marville, the present-day Post Office, and was often to be seen sitting outside on summer evening Panama hat on head and a fiddle ready to play. (The history of Bysbie Mill is told on page 61).

Gavie Cronie with his lorry and dog

When Gavie Cronie, Margaret's father, took over the house he was just beginning to build up a local transport business only to have his newest and best lorry commandeered for war service. But Gavie persisted and his business ran for many years handling local goods traffic.

Latterly one of his most important roles was to provide the vehicle for the Coastguard Life Saving Unit. Long before the advent of Coastguard stations, Land Rovers and two-way radios, Mr. Cronie provided an emergency 24 hour service. In his latter years Gavie also presided benevolently with Mrs. Cronie over the Post Office before it migrated to the Café and then back to its present home with Margaret Cronie.

To go back up the road to the Café, its most famous operator was undoubtedly Nan Love, together with husband Bill. Many village youngsters of that era will remember with affection, long before the days of youth clubs and television in the home, many winter evenings that saw half the village youth trying to make one Orangina and one plate of chips last the night.

Nan also allowed and provided background music on an ancient gramophone with equally historic records. *"She was only seven when she was called to heaven"* is one sentimental ballad that is recalled and Jo Stafford's ballads also trigger off memories.

Nan's family also ran the Castle both pre- and post-war as one of the few guesthouses. It was reputed that in busy summer spells the man of the house was dispatched to sleep in an outhouse.

Another guest house to be remembered – one of the few business premises in Tonderghie Row – was Crecy House which was run by the Curran and Larter families for 37 years. It memorably hosted the two Australian pilots whose job it was to fly – by radio control – the Tiger Moth planes for the anti-aircraft gunnery exercises.

Crecy House, in the foreground - seen in the early 1900's

Just below Marville, at Burnside, there were quite a number of "industrial units", to use a modern phrase. Not all of those have been recorded but there was certainly a blacksmith's shop and some carpentry and boatbuilding businesses. One of the more famous boat builders was Peter Crichton who, unusually for a builder of small craft, worked from models. His beautifully made scale models can still be seen in the Wigtown Bay Sailing Club. He was also distinguished by being involved in a rather dramatic breach of promise case.

Around and above the area of the Drummullin Burn the miller's pig sties once stood. His grandson can remember seeing them being fed live eels caught in the mill lade. In the post war seventies this became the marine engineering workshop and chandlery started by Keith Lonsdale and subsequently run by Bob Rowley.

Burnside, seen in the late 1920's

Going down further towards Windy Lane – where the street narrows before the Captain's Garden (and why did modern bureaucracy do away with the old street names?) – Netherton at one time was home to a sweet and toffee business run by Mrs. Milligan and later by Jenny Pringle. At about the same time, in the lane behind, a wooden hut was home to an ice-cream business run by the Lenaghan family.

'Windy Lane', with Captain's Garden on the left

In Windy Lane, at Netherton House, was the butcher's shop run by Joe Hale – his wife was a highly respected teacher. Across the road, in what is now the garage for the Captain's Garden, was a china shop run by Mrs. Andrew McWilliam – subsequently run from their main shop.

Moving on down the road, what was once the school became home to a carpenter's business run by Billy Lyons before its present day conversion to a private home. It is worth noting that almost opposite that entry, the early charts and maps show a carpenter's wood yard on the site where, history relates, the Church was subsequently built because the local landowners would not give permission for it to be built elsewhere. It may have been the wood yard for one of the many boat-building businesses over the years.

The McWilliam family were long established village residents as shipbuilders. The shipyard employed eight men and it was responsible for the building of a dozen ships. The street up to Coonan was known as Jib Boom Street because the bows of vessels under construction pointed there. Several craft of considerable

Shipbuilding at the Isle in the 1860's

size and importance in local history came from their yard. One of their first three-masted ships was to lead to the demise of the business on a voyage to South America - salt was used as ballast, and this ruined the valuable cargo of machinery. Claims against the yard resulted in its closing – the patent slipway was dismantled and sold to Carrickfergus – but the property found a new life as a grocery and general store with, later, a petrol station.

ISLE OF WHITEHORN.

Stories about the McWilliam family business are legion and nearly all stress the paternal way its proprietors behaved to the villagers. In the years of the Depression it is known that no one was allowed to go hungry and groceries often provided when there

The old slipway

was little hope of payment. John McWilliam, the last of the family to preside there, and also a former harbourmaster, was no exception and the village was a lot poorer for his passing and the eventual closure of the shop in 2000.

Residents and visitors still remember the quaint, leaning store where needles and anchors were probably standard items of stock.   The Architectural Heritage Society of Scotland considered the McWilliam Brothers store unique and deplored its demolition in 2001. The wooden letters on the side of the building were saved, and are now displayed in St Ninian's Hall.

9 - A Pleasant Place to do Business...

Behind the present Wigtown Bay Sailing Club was a garage business started and run by Jimmy Johnston, a marine engineer. It was then run by the Kelly family who, after a fire, moved to Whithorn and ran a garage business there.

On the harbour there was a blacksmith's shop where Jack Niblock now houses his boats and this was a near neighbour to the joiner's shop run by Alex Reid and subsequently sold to Sandy Faulds. He in turn continued a flourishing business, which he handed over to his son Alan.   Apart from the normal business as joiner and undertaker Alan continued the Isle's tradition by building boats, often on fibreglass hulls and of some size. The premises also had a claim to fame as one of the backgrounds used in the filming of '*The Wicker Man*' – a project which put quite a few pounds in the pockets of local people who appeared as extras – unaware of the way that this film would develop cult status.

When Alan retired the business was briefly run by Keith Lonsdale before becoming part of the Barr shop business and latterly being run by Anne and Eddie Richards as a top of the range children's clothes shop. Fergie and Isobel Harkness then ran a successful restaurant business there before it reverted to a private house.

Another howff with a long history comes next in the form of the Steam Packet Inn.   There were lots of other licensed premises in the village although few have been recorded.   But the Packet has survived the years and thrown up a lot of characters.   Brother and sister partnership Jimmy and Jessie Robertson bought the property around the turn of the century for a few hundred pounds.

Enjoying the harbour atmosphere at the Steam Packet today

Over the years they expanded to include the house next door, which had been the home of Captain Weaver's family – Jack Niblock's grandfather.   Jack's mother was born in what is now the hotel dining room.

Jimmy and Jessie owned the land behind the Packet – including St. Ninian's Chapel and the old lifeboat house.   He kept livestock there and by the time of his death also owned a considerable amount of village property.   A good oil painting of this famous old character still hangs in the hotel.

Noni Browne

When he retired, the hotel was taken over and considerably modernised by Colonel Kinnear Browne, in turn succeeded by his wife Noni, another personality remembered by many. She had very definite views over who was welcome or otherwise in her dining room. Many will also remember the two apricot poodles that formed an important part of the establishment. There was also Clara the parrot who unfortunately met a sticky end at the beaks of the gulls that did not care for this colourful intruder. When Noni retired the hotel was bought and again modernised by John and Sarah Scoular who now have son Alastair in charge.

Most of the rest of the harbour properties were tied to and run in connection with marine activities, particularly in its heyday as a seaport during the 19th Century when the trading schooners and the early paddle steamers bearing the name *Countess of Galloway* (there were three in the period 1824 – 1880) were the main source of transport for both people and goods.

This era ended with the coming of the railways, particularly when Whithorn was brought into the network. It was the beginning of a long period of decline.

The Isle Harbour seen on a postcard sent in 1911

A coal store, weighbridge and other commercial buildings saw a variety of owners, including the Duff family who were also notable ship owners. Most of the commercial buildings were taken over by James Wyllie as part of his agricultural service firm and after that passed through various hands.

9 - A Pleasant Place to do Business...

The old Customs House was an exception – for many years being owned and used by Bill Brown of Cutreoch.   Today, of course, things are constantly changing.   The Customs House had a very busy period as a shop in the ownership of the Barr family and is currently in process of being rebuilt, primarily as holiday accommodation.

The ownership of the harbour itself is an interesting piece of history bearing in mind its importance to the community and this is covered in the next chapter.   It was owned until the mid-nineteenth Century by Whithorn Town Council - probably as a legacy of the old Abbey holdings.   But when the Council went bust in the middle of the century it was taken over by a private harbour company whose shareholders and directors were purely local, mainly from the farming community headed by Bill Brown of Cutreoch and Morrach. That company also ran into problems when damage to the harbour called for repairs far beyond their means.

It is fair to say that with its renewal as a harbour, usable by both fishing and pleasure craft, the whole village benefited and moved forward.   The recent completion of the ambitious 'Ninian's Landing' project on the harbour, replacing the derelict grain stores, has restored a fine vista that recaptures the bygone glory of the Isle.

Enjoying the sun and the view at the back of McWilliam's store

10 – The Isle and the Sea

This major work was undertaken in 2002 by a group led by the late Dennis Fisher gathering historical material for the Isle's website.

Subsequent additions to the material have been contributed by John Scoular and Shaun McGuire

The Isle of Whithorn is now a haven for pleasure craft and a few fishing vessels, but in times past the village was an important harbour.

The earliest sign of habitation is the Iron Age fort where what we call the Cairn is now. Was it built there because of the shelter given by the bay? In those days water transport was probably by raft and coracle which were most likely used mainly for fishing, as there was not the need then to travel long distances - that came later.

We know that the Vikings came here and their settlement in Whithorn by the Abbey shows that they stayed for a long time. The Isle's bay would certainly have attracted them. St. Ninian came over from Cumbria and it is doubtful that he walked here, he almost certainly came by sea, and pilgrims landed here on their way to the religious community at Whithorn. At that time Whithorn Priory owned all of the surrounding land and the fish yard where the monks kept fish for their Friday meal can still be seen. After the Reformation most of the land and property belonging to the Priory was given to Whithorn Town Council. In 1663 the Scottish Parliament approved a Charter of Confirmation granting the village the status of a Royal Burgh. The Charter confirms that the Isle was a harbour at that time and also that it was considered to be part of Whithorn.

The relevant part of the Charter states: *". . . together with the shore or seaport of the same called the Isle of Whithorn which they have possessed beyond all memory of man in a free Burgh Royal, free harbour and shore within all the bounds of use and custom and is given. . . . etc. "*

During the 19th Century Whithorn Town Council became bankrupt and ownership of the harbour was transferred to a Trust owned by some local farmers and other worthies. Later still the County Council took over the harbour from the Trust. Very little is known about when the pier was constructed, but it is shown on the first ever chart of the Isle published in 1793, (see page 14). At that time the Cairn area was an island called, not surprisingly, the Isle of Whithorn, the rest of the village being called Whithorn. In 1793 the Isle was a base for the King's ships and Revenue cutters, and it was proposed to extend the pier to give added protection and to cut secondary exits out of the bay. These were not feasible because in a southerly wind the ships could not beat out of the bay, they had to warp themselves out using rings fitted into rocks on either side. The same situation would exist for these secondary exits. In bad weather a south easterly blows right into the harbour, and the bay becomes untenable for anchored vessels that would have had to come into the harbour for protection.

The Schooners and Packets

Until the coming of the railway the movement of people and goods was almost entirely by sea. The main type of vessel involved was the topsail schooner, ubiquitous maid of all work that carried passengers one day, coal or other goods the next, or all together at the same time. They were the buses and lorries of their time. A descendant of one of the schooner masters living in the village had the account books of his trading up and down the west coast of Scotland. It is interesting

to see that one particular year's trading resulted in a profit of £5! (in the 1900's, £5 was quite a lot of money).

One locally famous schooner was the *Ellen and Mary*, seen on the left. Her Master, Captain McGuffie, skippered her from the day that she was built until the time that she was broken up and the remains of her timbers still lie outside the house that he occupied in Port William.

When she was dismantled, Captain McGuffie (or his descendants), gave her figurehead to the Seamen's Mission in Ayr where it sat in the window for many years until it was moved to the Maritime Museum at Irvine. With the coming of steamships, a few schooners fitted with engines continued trading.

Another type of vessel that was a familiar sight in the Isle in the late 19th Century and up to the First World War was the oyster smack. These were large boats, 70-footers, which sailed up from Kent for the oyster fishing, but very few pictures of them seem to be in existence. A relic of those days can be found beyond the chalet development at Laigh Isle on the way up to Stein Head, where, in the first gully, there is a brick wall with holes in it which was the oyster keep. The smacks fished the oyster beds in both Wigtown and Luce Bays and landed their catches at the Isle of Whithorn.

Oyster smacks at the Isle, circa 1873

At least one Master remained, Captain Weaver of the *Winward*, who bought more schooners and traded all around here, to the Isle of Man, Ireland, and regularly to Liverpool. The Liverpool connection was very strong and there are still people in the Isle who have relatives living in that area. In due course the oysters were fished out, and in the late 1970's scallop dredgers came on the scene to fish the Queen scallop, or 'queenie'. Originally these had been thrown over the side, but by this time markets had been found for them both in Britain and on the Continent.

The death knell of the schooners was the coming of the steam packets, with several bearing the name *Countess of Galloway*. They took most of the trade away from the schooners, and in due course the railway came to Whithorn and that won over the business from the steam packets. The last *Countess of Galloway* was sold and briefly served on the short sea crossing to Northern Ireland.

The last schooner to visit the Isle in living memory was the *Alpha* which traded until World War II. A local resident remembers her coming into the harbour in 1939 carrying a cargo of coal that was discharged into a warehouse, now demolished, down at the harbour.

SS *Countess of Galloway* at the Isle of Whithorn, bound for Liverpool, in the late nineteenth century

Below - a busy evening at the Isle, July 2007

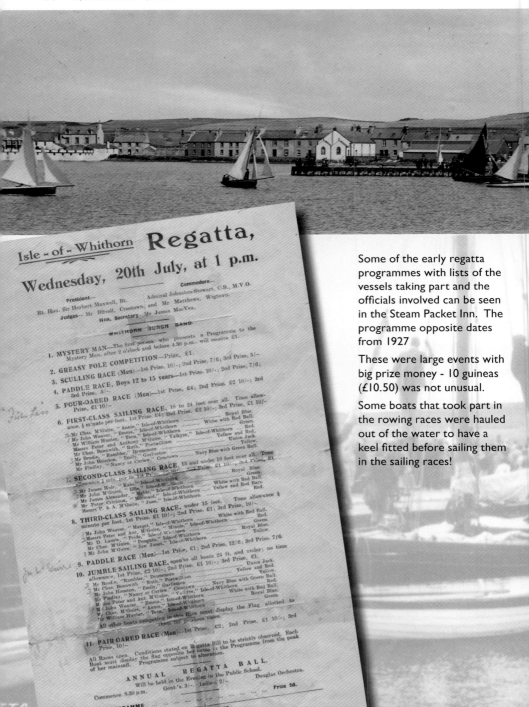

Isle-of-Whithorn Regatta,
Wednesday, 20th July, at 1 p.m.

President—
Rt. Hon. Sir Herbert Maxwell, Bt.   Admiral Johnston-Stewart, C.B., M.V.O.

Commodore—

Judges— Mr Birrell, Creetown, and Mr Matthews, Wigtown.

Hon. Secretary— Mr James MacVea.

WHITHORN BURGH BAND.

1. MYSTERY MAN.—The first person who presents a Programme to the Mystery Man, after 2 o'clock and before 4.30 p.m., will receive £1.

2. GREASY POLE COMPETITION—Prize, £1.

3. SCULLING RACE (Men)—1st Prize, 10/-; 2nd Prize, 7/6; 3rd Prize, 5/-

4. PADDLE RACE, Boys 12 to 15 years—1st Prize, 10/-; 2nd Prize, 7/6; 3rd Prize, 5/-.

5. FOUR-OARED RACE (Men)—1st Prize, £4; 2nd Prize, £2 10/-; 3rd Prize, £1 10/-.

6. FIRST-CLASS SAILING RACE, 18 to 24 feet over all. Time allowance, 1 minute per foot. 1st Prize, £4; 2nd Prize, £2 10/-; 3rd Prize, £1 10/-

1 Mr Chas. M'Guire, " Annie," Isle-of-Whithorn .... Royal Blue.
2 Mr John Weaver, " Emma," Isle-of-Whithorn .... White with Red Ball.
3 Mr William Hunter, " Tern," Isle-of-Whithorn .... Green.
  Messrs Peter and Anthony M'Guire, " Valkyre," Isle-of-Whithorn ... Yellow and Red.
4 Mr Chas. Bennwith, " Ruth," Portwilliam .... Union Jack.
5 Mr Brodie, " Rambler," Emily, Garlieston .... Yellow.
  Mr John Houston, " Nancy or Curlew," Creetown ...... Navy Blue with Green Ball.
  Mr Findlay, " Nancy or Curlew," Creetown

7. SECOND-CLASS SAILING RACE, 15 and under 18 feet over all. Time allowance 1 min. per ft. 1st Prize, £2; 2nd Prize, £1 10/-; 3rd Prize, £1

1 Mr James Muir, " Kate," Isle-of-Whithorn .... Royal Blue.
2 Mr John M'Guire, " Mabel," Isle-of-Whithorn .... Green.
3 Mr James Alexander, " Mermaid," Isle-of-Whithorn ...... White with Red Ball.
  Messrs T. & A. M'Guire, " Jane," Isle-of-Whithorn ...... Yellow and Red Bars.
  Mr Trevor Crickton, ... Red.

8. THIRD-CLASS SAILING RACE, under 15 feet. Time allowance ½ minute per foot. 1st Prize, £1 10/-; 2nd Prize, £1; 3rd Prize, 10/-.

1 Mr John Weaver, " Marget," Isle-of-Whithorn .... White with Red Ball.
2 Messrs Peter and Ant. M'Guire, " Minnie," Isle-of-Whithorn ... Red.
3 Mr D. Laurie, " Pride," Isle-of-Whithorn .... Green.
  Mr Chas. " Penguin," Isle-of-Whithorn .... Royal Blue.
4 Mr John M'Guire, " Jew Janet," Isle-of-Whithorn ...... Yellow.

9. PADDLE RACE (Men)—1st Prize, £1; 2nd Prize, 12/6; 3rd Prize, 7/6.

10. JUMBLE SAILING RACE, open to all boats 24 ft. and under; no time allowance. 1st Prize, £2 10/-; 2nd Prize, £1 10/-; 3rd Prize, £1.

1 Mr Brodie, " Rambler," Drummore .... Union Jack.
2 Mr Chas. Bennwith " Ruth " Portwilliam .... Yellow and Red.
3 Mr John Houston, " Emily," Garlieston .... Yellow.
  Messrs Peter and Ant. M'Guire, " Valkyre," Isle-of-Whithorn ... Navy Blue with Green Ball.
4 Mr Findlay, " Nancy or Curlew," .... Red.
5 Mr John Weaver, " Emma," Isle-of-Whithorn ...... White with Red Ball.
  Mr Chas. M'Guire, " Annie," Isle-of-Whithorn ...... Royal Blue.
  Mr William Hunter, " Tern," Isle-of-Whithorn ...... Green.

All other boats competing in this Race must display the Flag allotted to them in previous races.

11. PAIR OARED RACE (Men)—1st Prize, £2; 2nd Prize, £1 10/-; 3rd Prize, 10/-.

All Races open. Conditions stated on Regatta Bill to be strictly observed. Each Boat must display the flag opposite her name in the Programme from the peak of her mainsail. Programme subject to alteration.

ANNUAL REGATTA BALL.

Will be held in the Evening in the Public School.

Commence 8.30 p.m.   Gent.'s 3/-;   Ladies, 2/-.   Douglas Orchestra.

Price 2d.

Some of the early regatta programmes with lists of the vessels taking part and the officials involved can be seen in the Steam Packet Inn. The programme opposite dates from 1927

These were large events with big prize money - 10 guineas (£10.50) was not unusual.

Some boats that took part in the rowing races were hauled out of the water to have a keel fitted before sailing them in the sailing races!

The Regattas

Regattas have been a feature of the Isle of Whithorn for many years and probably date from the late 19th Century. Local dignitaries and their wives, all in their best suits and crinolines, would gather outside the gamekeeper's cottage before coming down to the harbour.

A very social occasion at a 1930's Regatta

In 1931 there was a tragedy when two competitors lost their lives and as a result there were no further regattas before the outbreak of the Second World War. They resumed in 1945, and since then they have been held every year, going from strength to strength, and now lasting over two days.

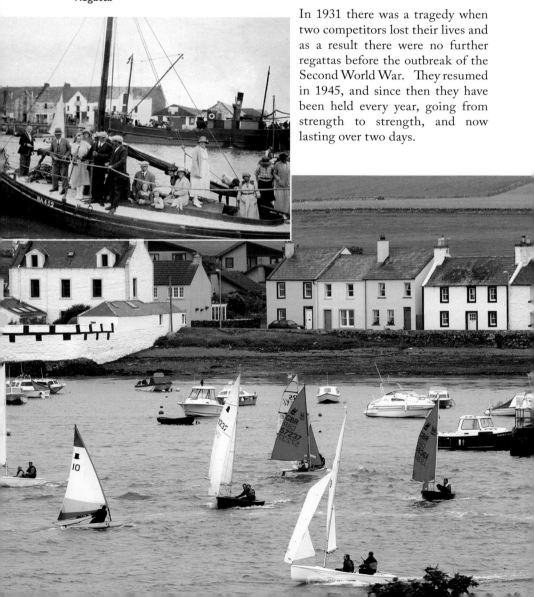

The Lifeboats

On the way to the Cairn, there are the remains of an old building - all that is left of the old lifeboat house. When it was cleaned up to accommodate the Witness Cairn, a cobbled floor, with runners on which the wheels of the lifeboat bogie ran, was revealed.

The building had a roof until well after the Second World War although the station was closed in 1919, when a motor lifeboat was placed on station at Kirkcudbright.

The Lifeboat Station was set up in 1869 in the days when lifeboats were not fitted with engines and had to be rowed. This meant that if the casualty was in Wigtown Bay it was a long row against invariably strong tides. In those circumstances the lifeboat was hauled through the village, past Isle Farm and down to Cairnhead, where there is still a wide gate leading to a small shore, from where the lifeboat was launched.

The Isle's third lifeboat, George & Margaret is launched at the Chapel Port

Taking the boat through the village was a major task, not least because there were houses standing on what is now the car park by the telephone box, resulting in a very tight turn into the Portyerrock road. The bogie had enormous iron wheels, and because of the difficulty of rounding the corner a granite pillar was erected at the corner of the end house so that the bogie could be pivoted round it without causing damage.

It's believed that when the maroon was fired the local farmers were each required to send three pairs of horses in case it was necessary to take the boat to Cairnhead.

Hauling the lifeboat through Main Street to Cairnhead for a launch

During the half-century that the lifeboat station was operating there were three lifeboats: *Charlie Peake* (1869 - 1886), 7 launches and 10 lives saved; *Henry and John Leighton* (1886 - 1901), 12 launches and 22 lives saved; *George and Margaret* (1901 - 1919), six launches and six lives saved. In all, 25 launches and 38 lives saved. After the station closed, the boat was sold off for £50 in 1920. Closure in 1919 was due as much to the lack of a launching crew rather than the availability of a boat.

Lifeboat coverage was transferred to the Kirkcudbright Station, but this was not always ideal, even when sail was overtaken by power, because a shallow bar on the River Dee impeded passage.

Today, with the advent of fast modern craft, lifeboat coverage is extensive. The RNLI at Kirkcudbright is notably aided by PIRSAC (Port William Inshore Rescue Services Action Committee), a locally run and independently funded inshore craft based at Port William, which can be moved by road to all parts of the area in an emergency. If necessary, additional support from lifeboats stationed at Ramsey and Peel in the Isle of Man can be summoned by the Coastguard Service HQ in Liverpool. Additionally, air-sea rescue can be undertaken by the RAF and Royal Navy with Sea King helicopters.

May 2005: The RNLI Kirkcudbright lifeboat assists a local fishing boat into harbour - the Isle Coastguard team maintaining watch from the Cairn

The people of the Isle have always been very supportive of sea rescue services. The community has its own fundraising branch of the RNLI - a group of volunteers whose efforts regularly raise around £5,000 each year. PIRSAC, whose team are seen exercising above, is similarly supported by fund-raising events.

Coastguards

For many years the Coastguard presence in the Isle, as with most coastal villages, was a branch of the Customs and Revenue – they were more interested in catching smugglers than saving lives. The present day coastguards in the village started in 1937. The first Station Officer of the team was John McGuire and the equipment was kept in a wee shed on the Cairn, behind the sailing clubhouse. After getting fed up of trudging through what was a mud hole at the time, to reach the shed, he gave the Coastguards use of a small piece of land beside the Drummullin Burn bridge to build a garage to store the equipment.

Isle of Whithorn
Rescue Company
pictured about
1939

In those days one of the main duties of the Coastguard teams was 'watchkeeping' - to keep an eye on shipping in the area in order to ensure the safety of those at sea.

This practice continued up to the 1970's in a purpose-built watchtower on Stein Head. The garage at the bridge contained the equipment used to rescue people from boats in difficulty on the coastline. A rocket with a line attached was fired over the ship in distress and the crew used the line to haul out the heavy rope, onto which the coastguard team attached a Breeches Buoy. This was an ingenious contraption, best described as a lifebuoy with a pair of heavy canvas shorts attached. The crew of the stricken vessel took turns at sitting in this vital piece of equipment and being hauled in to the shore to safety by the Coastguard team.

Transporting the lifesaving equipment to wherever it was required was left to the discretion of the team, no vehicle being provided. A vital member of any Coastguard team in Britain was the local lorry owner! The Isle team was no different and older members of the community may remember seeing the sixteen-man team and all their equipment poised precariously on the back of Gavie Cronie's lorry as they sped off to a rescue. When John McGuire retired he was succeeded as Station Officer by his son Ernie, and when Gavie Cronie sold his lorry the duty of transporting the team and equipment passed to Alex Steele, using Carson's coal lorry, which he drove in his 'day job'. The much bigger lorry held the team and equipment with ease, although some of the distressed mariners must have thought it bizarre when the team coming to their aid arrived covered in coal dust! When Alex retired the transport duties were taken over by Willie Murdoch, who had bought the coal business.

One of the most important tasks in effecting a rescue was firing the rocket and line. The last member of the Isle team to perform this duty was Martin McGuire and he was as good as they come. Firing a rocket over a ship or boat, which was bouncing around on rocks in a gale of wind was a very difficult job, especially using a rocket launcher mounted on a flimsy tripod.

Mental calculations had to be done quickly to allow for the effect the wind would have on the rocket. Martin never needed more than two shots at it, and usually hit the target first go. All the Coastguard teams in the area used to take part in an annual competition, which involved firing the rocket, setting up the Breeches Buoy equipment and recovering a casualty. The Isle team won this competition on a regular basis.

Perhaps the finest hour of the Isle Coastguard team occurred in 1969. A small coaster, the *Uranus*, was driven ashore on Eggerness Point at Garlieston in a severe gale and blizzard. The team had to battle their way through blizzards and snow drifts to Garlieston, using the coal lorry and John McWilliam's van. Upon arrival they discovered that they could not get anywhere near the vessel with the vehicles, so they had to carry the heavy equipment almost a mile before they could set up. When the breeches buoy was sent out to the coaster the foreign crew, who spoke little English, refused to come ashore. The team stood by, waiting for the inevitable. The frozen team sent out a message to the skipper, informing him that if he and his crew didn't come ashore now, they were leaving. The note also explained that they would return in the morning and recover them 'either dead or alive' and that the team weren't bothered either way as they had an undertaker in the team!

The rescue team eventually got a signal to haul in the breeches buoy. When they got it ashore they discovered a bottle of brandy and a carton of cigarettes secured in the canvas shorts. This was much appreciated by the extremely cold team. As the weather deteriorated further the ship's crew consented to be rescued from the ship, which was bouncing around alarmingly on the rocks. The first casualty recovered was the skipper's heavily pregnant wife, who was particularly pleased to get her feet on solid ground! The entire crew were rescued and the Isle team was awarded the Board of Trade Wreck Service Shield. This annual award was given for the best service rendered to casualties at sea, and is a great source of pride to the Isle team to this day.

Station Officer Alan Faulds (right) receives the Board of Trade Wreck Service Shield in 1969

Michael McGuire and Jimmy Hannah receive their Long Service Awards in 2006

Two members of the current Coastguard team, Jimmy Hannah and Michael McGuire, were involved in the rescue – although they were both too young to be official members of the team. Alan Faulds, who was also at the *Uranus* rescue, became the next Station Officer and in 1986 presided over the move to a new Coastguard station in Boyach Road. Alan led the team through a period of change, which saw the removal of the breeches buoy equipment and the development of cliff rescue as one of the main duties of Coastguards. When Alan retired, he was succeeded by Andy Carnochan. It is testament to Andy's popularity and ability as team leader that, on his sudden and untimely death, Coastguards from as far apart as Kirkcudbright and Liverpool attended his funeral. The tragic loss of the *Solway Harvester* and all her crew touched the Coastguard team heavily as the skipper, Craig Mills, and his brother Robin were former members of the team and their cousin David was a serving member.

Generations of family members have served the Isle Coastguard team. The Station Officer today is Ernie McGuire's son, Shaun. For a small village the Isle can take pride in the fact that it has always been able to supply a team when much larger places have struggled to do so.

The Wrecks

The exposed coasts around Galloway have claimed many ships, particularly schooners around the turn of the century. Peter C Miller's book *'Galloway Shipwrecks'* catalogues around 35 vessels lost along the coastline from Portyerrock Bay to Burrowhead between 1812 and 1923, and this list is probably not exhaustive.

SS *Vanderbyl* is wrecked at the Screens, in December 1879

The best known is the *Chile*. This German owned ship was one of a class of sailing vessels built for the Chilean nitrate trade and was, unfortunately, in Liverpool at the start of the First World War. She was on passage to Glasgow as a prize when she went on shore just beyond St. Ninian's Cave at what is known as the Ladies Steps.

The then Captain Weaver led the crew to safety up the Ladies Steps, as a result of which the grateful crew presented him with a picture of the ship which now hangs in the Wigtown Bay Sailing Clubhouse. The *Chile* was big, her masts could be seen above the cliffs, and it is alleged that the people of the Isle were never wont to waste things, so much of the furnishings of the ship found their way into the village, even saloon doors, which made excellent back doors to some houses!

Another wreck is that of the *Inkosi*, a steamship which was sunk off the coast during World War I by a German submarine.

SS Inkosi

Two families remember their parents telling them that they sat on the Cairn and watched the action. The vessel was torpedoed and the submarine then surfaced to sink it by gunfire after allowing the Captain and 47 crew members and passengers to take to the boats. The survivors rowed ashore and were put up in the village school. The wreck lay undisturbed for many years as she is in deep water. In the past few years, as more advanced equipment has become generally available, it has been possible for amateur divers to reach the wreck. Sadly, this pursuit has not been without loss of life here.

Darent burns in the Isle bay after being towed in

In 1922 the fishing vessel *Darent* caught fire four miles off Cairnhead. James McCutcheon of the Isle went out and towed it into the bay, but unfortunately as she was petrol/paraffin powered the fire became uncontrollable and the vessel burned down to the waterline.

Portyerrock Bay is the final resting place of the steamer *Jasper*. Here lies a tragic story all too typical of marine history round our coasts. On the morning of 12th December 1888, farm workers and a local postman reported the masts of a vessel – still with masthead lights showing – less than a mile offshore from Dinnans farm. This was found to be the steamer *Jasper*, owned by Robertsons of Glasgow, which was on passage with a cargo of iron rail loaded at Whitehaven. It was reported to have been foggy weather at the time of the shipwreck and it was assumed that she had struck the rocks on the shore, where her propeller and rudder were later found, before foundering close by. Twice, local residents reported that they had heard a foghorn. Sadly, all the crew appeared to have perished and the only body to come ashore was that of Captain McNicol.

A tombstone was erected in Whithorn churchyard by the ship's owners. History tells of various unsuccessful attempts to salvage the cargo and the vessel itself. All these gave rise to a lovely local legend that when divers went down and looked through a porthole all the crew were sitting at the table – drowned. Proof of the view that local fact can soon become local fiction. For many years this wreck has been a well-known to both anglers and divers. For the underwater fraternity it has provided an ideal training ground in sheltered, shallow water. As she is encrusted in attractive marine growth she is quite a spectacular sight.

The Harbour Collapse

After the Second World War, the end of the pier was a pile of rubble - the years had not been kind to it. When James Wyllie bought the stores on the harbour he smoothed over the rubble and put a skin of concrete over the surface. It stayed like that until 1969 when, after a bad storm, it was seriously damaged.

Water pressure built up inside the pier and it was described as "looking like a jelly with a jigsaw on top" - huge chunks broke off. The cause apparently was that the pier had been pointed, but the top had not been sealed so that water got in, and built up until the wall just exploded.

Having the pier rebuilt was a major political battle. Alex Niblock, a prominent resident of the village, and Mr D. R. Wilson, Clerk to the Wigtown County Council, joined forces to try and get the pier rebuilt. Mr Wilson had the ability to argue and justify a case, and he was convinced that the pier needed to be rebuilt. He got the resources from St.Andrew's House, (in those days the Scottish Office), on the grounds of coastal protection: if it was not rebuilt, the lower parts of the village would be washed away. The official estimate of the cost was £65,000 but the rebuilding cost a lot more than that. It was said that the result was an increase of a penny in the pound on the rates.

Damage to the harbour after the 1972 storm

The scene at the Isle-of-Whithorn on Sunday morning as "The Sappers" continue with Operation Patch-up. (G–

ROYAL ENGINEER VOLUNTEERS SHO–
HARBOUR WALL WITH 800

Soldiers and Wigtown County Council workers piled 800 tons of rock into the damaged harbour wall at the Isle of Whithorn this week, and succeeded in keeping back this week's high tides. Only minor damage was caused to the pier head.

About 70 Territorials from the 71st Royal Engineers arrived at the Isle on Saturday and with the help of earth moving equipment and a fleet of County Council trucks carrying rock from local quarries they started to fill up the massive gaps in the harbour wall.

After four days continual work the men, who had been involved in the rescue of flooding victims at Weymouth in 1968, had completed their emergency measures.

It was on Tuesday with a 29 foot tide and a gale force wind whipping up the seas that the wall took its biggest battering. The villagers feared for their safety but the repaired quayside stood firm.

As the soldiers prepared to leave on Wednesday the villagers were full of pr– and were very – calm sea.

They had alr– appreciation of t– the soldiers, who – the village hall, – two barrels of be–

The local counc– W. Brown, said: "– not been filled go– what would have h– he added that it – a temporary job on – it would have to be – erly. "Without the ha– ing is of any use".

Village That Waits In Fear

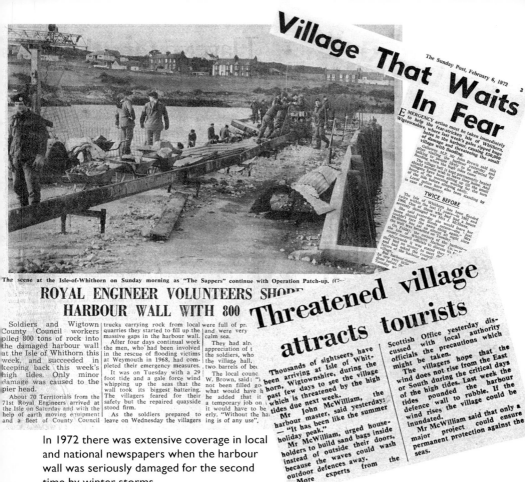

The Sunday Post, February 6, 1972 3

EMERGENCY action must be taken immediately to help the fear-stricken Isle of Whithorn, Wigtownshire, where last week's gales ripped huge holes in the harbour, causing £50,000 of damage and threatening the small village with flooding.

Galloway M.P. Mr John Brewis said this after visiting the harbour yesterday and talking to people likely to be affected by flooding when the high tides come.

The village hall is kept permanently heated should anyone wish to leave their home. And villagers have been sitting up till the small hours of the morning waiting for the turn of the tide before sleeping easily.

Local police have also been standing by in case of emergency.

TWICE BEFORE

The Isle of Whithorn has been flooded twice within the last 11 years—in 1961 and 1966. One of those who had had a house severely damaged was Mrs J. McShane.

She said yesterday she would leave her home should the floods return—she "just couldn't face the same thing again." Mrs McShane has sat up almost all night since the wall was breached on Tuesday.

On Friday, the owners of the harbour—the Isle of Whithorn Harbour Co.—m– county council officials to discuss its f–

Afterwards it was stated they – they had no money to meet th– and had asked the council – future of the harbour and – village.

But harbour-maste– he saw very little – done before th– Tuesday w–

Threatened village attracts tourists

Thousands of sightseers have been arriving at Isle of Whithorn, Wigtownshire, during the past few days to see the village which is threatened by the high tides due next week.

Mr John McWilliam, the harbour master, said yesterday: "It has been like the summer holiday peak."

Mr McWilliam, urged householders to build sand bags inside instead of outside their doors, because the waves could wash outdoor defences away.

More experts from the Scottish Office yesterday discussed with local authority officials the precautions which might be taken.

The villagers hope that the wind does not rise from the East or South during the critical days of the high tides. Last week the tides pounded the harbour defence wall to rubble. If the wind rises the village could be inundated.

Mr McWilliam said that only a major project could ensure permanent protection against the seas.

In 1972 there was extensive coverage in local and national newspapers when the harbour wall was seriously damaged for the second time by winter storms

The Disasters

All seaports and harbours have histories that tell of disasters and tragedies and the Isle of Whithorn is no exception. One such incident occurred in 1931 when the annual regatta was cancelled due to bad weather, and unfortunately some hardy souls decided to race in any case. One of the boats capsized, and instead of staying with the boat and waiting for rescue, the three crew members decided to swim for the shore. Two of them died, and as a result there were no more regattas until after the Second World War.

The Isle has had more than its fair share of fishing disasters in recent years. In 1986 Willie Pagan was lobster fishing off Port William when he ran into problems with his engine, but instead of waiting for assistance he decided to swim ashore and was drowned in the process.

"And quiet sleep and a sweet dream when the long trick's over"

John Masefield

In Memory Of The Crew Of The Solway Harvester
Lost With All Hands Off The Isle Of Man 11th January 2000

Robin Scott Mills — Aged 33 years
Andrew Craig Mills — Aged 29 years
Martin Hugh Milligan — Aged 26 years
John Doyle Murphy — Aged 22 years
David Mills — Aged 18 years
Wesley John Jolly — Aged 17 years
David Joseph Lyons — Aged 17 years

"And Quiet Sleep And A Sweet Dream When The Long Trick's Over"
John Masefield

January 2004
Dedication of the *Solway Harvester* Memorial

The Solway Harvester

A major disaster occurred on 11th January 2000, which devastated the village and surrounding communities. In treacherous Force 9 conditions the scallop dredger *Solway Harvester* was making for shelter at Ramsey on the Isle of Man when it disappeared with all of its crew. Craig Mills, the skipper; his brother Robin, and their cousin David all came from the Isle. Of the remaining crew, three came from Whithorn and one from Garlieston. The vessel had obviously gone down fast for both of the liferafts were subsequently found unopened.

The village was in shock and the tragedy and its aftermath received much coverage from the media. The Prime Minister expressed his sympathy in the House of Commons and a message of condolence was received from the Queen. Journalists and television crews descended upon the village in strength, causing some friction with their intrusiveness. Later, the Duke of Rothesay, Prince Charles, came at his own request to meet the bereaved families.

The reason for the sinking was a mystery and various theories were put forward such as a collision with a submarine or a floating container washed off another vessel. The UK Government was unwilling to finance the raising of the *Solway Harvester* to try and determine the reason for the sinking, but the village will always be grateful to the Isle of Man Government for agreeing to meet that cost.

In early February 2000, divers recovered the bodies of the seven crew members, and their funerals took place on 9th February. The Whithorn and Garlieston crew members were buried at private ceremonies in the morning. In the afternoon the three Isle victims were buried after what must have been one of the largest funerals ever seen in the village. The Isle Church was reserved for families and close friends who overflowed outside, and the service was relayed to another gathering in the village hall as well as a large number of people in the road outside. Reports estimated that there were in the region of 1500 mourners.

The lifting of the *Solway Harvester* was repeatedly delayed due to bad weather and was finally completed on 27th June after which investigations into the sinking were commenced by the Isle of Man Police and the Marine Accident Investigation Branch. The collision theory was not supported by the investigations, and subsequently the owners of the vessel were taken to Court - an action that is still continuing at the time of compiling this book in 2010.

Another tragedy occurred on 13th March 2003 when Sam Archer, a local Isle fisherman, was lost in the Solway, along with his boat. No reason for the accident has been discovered; some personal possessions were found soon after he disappeared and eventually his body was recovered from the sea off Whitehaven on 5th July the same year.

Looking out towards the Perch

The Perch

A reef of rock runs out from the west side of the mouth of the bay, and can be a hazard to craft coming into the Isle. For many years the end of this reef was marked with an iron pole, erected by the Harbour Board after they took over the harbour from Whithorn Town Council. It is interesting to read the account which was rendered by Archibald McDowell *"for the erection of the perch at the Screens at the Isle of Whithorn"*:

"To Robb Mills for boring 4 holes with hammer and chisel for 4 stays and inserting the spliced wire lugs for stays – 16 shillings. To John McGovern for labouring for Robb Mills – 9 shillings. To A.D. McDowell for erecting steel perch with the assistance of said two men – one pound and threepence".

The Northern Lights helicopter takes the Perch towards the reef

Eventually the perch was bent by a severe storm and it remained like that for many years. Ultimately it collapsed in another storm giving rise to a great argument about who was responsible for replacing it. The Wigtown Bay Sailing Club tried to mark it with a buoy without success; the District Council claimed that it was not their responsibility, and eventually the Northern Lighthouse Board, who are responsible for navigational aids in Scotland, were persuaded against their better judgment to erect a new perch. This new structure was erected with the aid of helicopters at a cost of £25,000 and needless to say it was not in place for very long before it got knocked down. The old one had stood there for years and years…! It was replaced, again at a cost of £25,000 - and once more it was hit. This time the repair was going to cost £13,000 and Northern Lights decided that enough was enough.

Maritime Families

With so much of its income and so many jobs coming from the sea it is not surprising that this shaped the architecture and layout of the village over the last two centuries.

Local folk looked to Liverpool for work getting there either by the schooners or latterly the Steam Packet. At the turn of the century it is estimated that there were about fifty holders of Master's certificates living in and around the village.

There now remains living in the village only one Master Mariner in Captain Jack Niblock, although others hold engineering qualifications. Jack went to sea in what was then a very traditional way – as a "Brass Bounder" or cadet apprenticed to one of the great Liverpool companies – the famous Blue Funnel Line. It was a line to which many local people owed jobs – there is a corner in a local graveyard which is still known as "Blue Funnel Corner".

Capt. Jack Niblock

Jack came from a sea-faring family – his grandfather, Captain Weaver, was Head Coastguard for many years. The family originally came from Kent but owned several vessels in local trade, the best known being the ketch *Winward*.

One of the leading captains of this vintage era was Captain James Learmonth whose book, "*Master in Sail*", became something of a clipper classic. The name of his best known command, the *Ben Gairn*, lives on today in the form of a Trust provided by one of his descendants, and which sponsors local young people on an annual opportunity for a trip on a sail training vessel.

Ketch *Winward*

Another leading Master Mariner was Captain Ross T. Jenkins, whose picture and a copy of his Master's ticket is on show in the Steam Packet. Although born in Ireland, Captain Jenkins built a fine house in Tonderghie Row and lived there until his death in 1916. His descendants still hold important memorabilia of his career.

The Robbs were another well known Isle family, Captain Robb being master of the schooner *Tonderghie*, owned in partnership with the Stewarts of Tonderghie.   Again, family documents in the archives of one of his descendants, Hugh Jaques, are important in history, including the financial record of an entire year's trading up and down the west coast.   The profit on the year was £5 - a lot for the time.   A latter day Captain Tom Robb was the last person in the village to hold a ticket in both sail and steam.

There were many other well-known seafarers over this period, including the Bie family who operated schooners in both Wigtownshire and the Stewartry and who have family living locally.

Capt. Thomas Robb

Captain Morrison, who built the two houses just below the Queen's Arms, was another clipper skipper and his relations still have a "potty chair" – known in the family as the Cape Horn chair because in those days whole families often travelled on the long voyages.

Another family with strong nautical connections were the Hunters, who first became established in the village in the 18th Century. Many of them were seafarers with Masters' tickets spread over three generations.   The last Hunter resident was a very well-known local character up to until his death in 1973.   He was a master of multi-tasking, holding various posts simultaneously including those of Postmaster, Postie, Beadle, Harbourmaster and, as the first and only car owner he stood in as taxi driver!   John actually had a row of hats for every job, hung inside his front door, and he would change his hats every time he changed tasks.

John and Mary Hunter

The McWilliam family spanned several generations. They started with shipbuilding at the Isle, and later ran the famous leaning wooden store and shop by the harbour right up to the end of the 20th Century.   Their story of enterprise can be found in Chapter 9.

No mention of village sea-farers would be complete without an outline of the McGuire dynasty. Their local founder was Martin McGuire, known as "The Bee" who migrated to the Isle all the way from Whithorn, via Portyerrock, before the Great War.   His sons carried on a fishing tradition that continues today – John, father of Martin and Ernie, was Head Coastguard for many years and his brothers Peter and Anton also fished from the Isle.   Another brother, Charlie, fished for many years

John McGuire

from the famous black huts at the Lag, at Monreith.   Other family members are still in the fishing industry today including the present Isle Harbourmaster, Shaun McGuire.

Ernie McGuire

The earliest known photo of the Isle School, taken in 1909.

Below: the Isle School photograph in 1972, taken six years before its closure.

11 – Schooldays in the Isle

Two former pupils of the Isle School, Lillias and Billy Brown, both residents of the village, look back on their schooldays.

In 1881 there were about 57 pupils in the school with two teachers. If the roll increased a pupil teacher or monitor was taken on. A School Board or locally elected people acted as Governors. The Chairman of the Board paid regular visits to check the registers and the pupils' work. An officer appointed by the Board visited every week to check the attendance and give 'drill' – physical education in the playground, weather permitting!

Attendance was a big problem, with pupils often absent without permission. Various reasons were given for this - whelk gathering, hoeing and thinning turnips in the spring, the grain harvest in September, followed by potato gathering in October. No doubt these tasks helped to augment the family income.

The pupils received instruction in reading and writing, arithmetic, English grammar and composition, dictation, geography and history, music, nature study and Religious Instruction. The girls had sewing, knitting and cooking, and the boys did woodwork.

The school year ran from March to February, and each year there were Government exams in every subject, before pupils were moved on to the next grade. The parish minister gave religious education exams regularly. Pupils not moving on to higher education stayed in the school and were given extra education in woodwork, cookery and gardening. The more able pupils had instruction in Latin, French and mathematics. The School Board set holidays. From 1902, Good Friday and Easter Monday were holidays. Throughout the year a one-day holiday would be granted – these days off were for various reasons:

> Farm roups – Stannock in 1882; Drummoral in 1884;
> Sunday School picnics;
> a one-day trip to the Isle of Man, June 1893;
> Launch of the new lifeboat, 1886;
> Regattas;
> Horse Shows in Newton Stewart;
> Whithorn Flower Show in 1885;
> In frosty weather, a half-day for sliding!

Until 1899 there was a one-day holiday in February for Whithorn Fast Day and a Victoria Day holiday in May. Later this became Empire Day and the children were given a lesson on the Union Flag.

By 1900, the school roll had increased to over 90 and there were three teachers. After the Great War ended in 1918 there were only two and this situation continued until 1973. At the beginning of the Second World War children were evacuated to the village from Glasgow. There were also some private evacuees who had come to stay with relatives. During this time the local children and Glasgow children each attended school for an half a day from 8 am to 1pm and 1pm to 5pm on alternate weeks. However the class teachers were still responsible for pupils during normal school hours – hence plenty of nature study and games out of doors!

Lillias Brown enjoys delving into the Isle's history, and who has helped compile this chapter.

From the 1930's to the seventies a Physical Education advisor visited the school to give instruction in PE. In the 1960's a music teacher came each week. Instruction was also given in cycling proficiency, and Certificates awarded. The Headmistress took her class to the sea for swimming lessons. School meals started in the 1960's – progress from a bowl of soup for a halfpenny (old pence) in 1911! The school roll began to drop through the sixties, and on the retirement of the assistant teacher in 1973, Primary 6 and 7 were transferred to Whithorn School, with the Isle continuing as a one-teacher school. When the Headmistress retired in 1977 it was closed for good. The building was sold and became a joiner's workshop. Then, in 2001, it was sold again and converted to a dwelling house.

Back in 1933 the Isle must have seemed a world apart. It was that year when Billy Brown, the younger of two sons born at Drummoral Farm, and blissfully unaware of the grim unfolding of the Nazi regime in 'distant' Europe, would set out from home, head down the stony track to the Burrowhead road, and turn left to walk down to the Isle.

A five-year old walking, occasionally with his brother, through most weathers? No school buses or 4 x 4's in those days! But what a wealth of things to see, hear, and even savour on the way to and from the Isle School.

"I never remember having to rush to school," said Billy, "there was always so much to see – and it was always different. " Coming from a farming family would have heightened that awareness of the countryside – in early spring the burst of creamy white blackthorn blossom, followed by the intense covering of yellow on the whins. "In summertime the road used to get so hot that we walked in bare feet – the tar got soft, and we loved to burst the bubbles with our toes!"

Going past the dairyman's cottage at Cutreoch, with the sounds of duck and waterfowl on Boyach Loch, the next point of interest was Rosies Brae. "I never knew who 'Rosie' was, but I remember seeing a small part of a ruin that would have been the cottage, and close by where Audrey Simpson's driveway is now." Billy also recalls that just opposite here were the tanks and filters that took the Isle's water supply from Boyach Loch.

Billy Brown enjoys a fine day's stroll retracing the walk from his former home at Drummoral to the Isle school.

But Rosies Brae itself was something quite different, and for Billy, intriguing. On the way home it was a 'must see' for once this had been a quarry, but in time it had become the community's rubbish dump. No houses here in those days of course. The first building would be Crecy House, home of Tommy Larter, one of the village worthies who could always be called on to organise local events.

Virtually all the houses in the Isle were occupied then and the distinctive, linear community of Tonderghie Row provided Billy with useful neighbourly knowledge: "At Roscairn, next door to Crecy, there was Mrs Findlay, who organised the Rural. During the war years, when many evacuees came to the Isle, she helped with their billeting, and also at the WVS Canteen on the harbour." Billy's walks to the Isle school were to continue until 1939, and he remembers well the sight of troops progressing up Tonderghie Row to Burrowhead Camp, having marched all the way from the old railway station in Whithorn.

"At No 35 there was Mrs Martin – she organised the Sunday School and made sure that every youngster in the Isle got a Christmas present. I remember asking for a torch, and actually getting one!" Next door was the Old Manse, its incumbent Minister, the Rev. Alan Kinnear would often help at harvest time, bringing in the sheaves.

The Tonderghie Row skyline is distinctive and little changed from the 1930's. A few roofs have been raised here and there to give much needed living space. Billy remembers particularly well Maggie McColm at Minnoch Cottage. Maggie's organ-playing was almost legendary – her sixpence donation and a peppermint at her side for the Sunday Service. But it was her deafness that brought a memorable quality to organ accompaniments for hymns – rarely did singers and organist finish in unison!

And so, round the corner and past the Queens, with the Post Office just across the lane that lead to Bysbie Mill. When he was older, Billy would work Saturday mornings at the mill, bruising oats. Over the bridge at Drummullin Burn, past Low Isle House, and then in front of the now lost cottages that made up Glasserton Row. "At one end lived Maggie Bell, and she would give me my lunch every school day," Billy says wistfully – "It's a shame the attractive row was demolished, I remember they had superb gardens – thanks to great quantities of peat which came from ships' ballasts, the soil was magnificent."

But time is pressing, and Billy must hurry along or risk the penalty of being late. He passed the house where John Hunter resided and made sure that everything in the village ticked – his main job was the Postman, but he was also the Church Beadle, the Water Bailiff and the Hallkeeper!

A 1920's view looking up Tonderghie Row towards Rosie's Brae and the Old Manse

Rounding the corner through the School Slap, the bell is ringing its 9 am summons to learning. Miss Paterson, Billy's first teacher, would be welcoming her charges for the day. The girls would assemble at the front door of the school, and the boys would gather at the back. Miss Paterson was very keen on Scottish country dancing. Billy, like his older brother John, became part of a small team of four girls and four boys from the Isle school that took part in the Newton Stewart Festival. "It was a thoroughly enjoyable time, and we got a day off school as well," mused Billy.

Miss Gass (later Mrs Hale) took over when Miss Paterson moved to Sorbie – and Billy remembers her as "a quiet teacher, but she kept our attention. History was my best subject, even though it wasn't Scottish history. Somehow I managed to get by in English! There were no Playstations in those days – marbles and conkers kept us amused at break time. And the school sports were held on the field which is where the Laigh Isle chalets are today."

When Billy looks over his garden wall to the Stinking Port and the small island that remains in the middle at high tide, he's reminded of the time when, with a few pals, he was marooned there in full view of the school. Unable to get back to shore, a boat was sent for, and Jack McGuire rowed around the Cairn to rescue them. Back on dry land there was retribution in store. "Oh, we all got the strap for that escapade," he recalled, "but it was fun, as were the rest of my schooldays."

The Isle School in 1934, with young Billy Brown in the front row, 2nd from right.

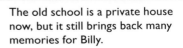

The old school is a private house now, but it still brings back many memories for Billy.

Very visible on the high ground at the landward end of the village is the Castle.   It is one of the last of the fortified houses to be built in Scotland at a time when there was beginning to be less open warfare between neighbours.

It is best defined as a 17th Century L-plan tower house. Initially thought to be a property of the Houstons of Drummaston, probably its best known early tenant was Sir John Reid who headed the Revenue squadron stationed locally to try to halt the activities of the flourishing "Free Traders".   He was responsible for a number of alterations to the Castle in the 1830's – not all of them considered improvements.

The Stewarts of Physgill then held titular ownership until February 1951, when the Castle and Spa Cottage were acquired - in what manner it is better not to surmise, although card games have been mentioned – by James Robertson. He was a larger than life character and landlord of the Steam Packet whose portrait hangs on the wall of the lounge bar to this day.   Over this period it was run as a comfortable if not sophisticated guest house.   On Jimmy's death the property was bought by the late Dr. William McAdam.

Harbour, Isle of Whithorn.

Two views of the harbour at the Isle - above the early 1920's, the picture below was taken in May 2010

The solicitor who handled the transaction, the late Davie Breckenridge, walked the boundaries with the purchaser and concluded by lifting a sod of earth and placing it in Dr. McAdam's hand – the last trace of a traditional Scottish practice connected with "sasine", or transfer of property. The Castle is now in the hands of one of Dr. McAdam's descendants and a much loved family home.

For those who prospered, many put their money into bricks and mortar – no different today – and some of the finest of the village houses built up to the time of the last war were memorials to sea-going ancestors.

From his eyrie on Rosie's Brae the late Douglas Lester, one of the village's most gently perceptive senior citizens, looked out over a village that changed much in the many years he knew it. Not that he resented change: "Some of the more recent residents don't realize how life was then, especially in the pre- and post war years. Life was quite difficult for many ordinary folk. Jobs were not easy to find and farming was by no means prosperous," he recalled. He remembered with affection picnic and swimming parties at the little bays on the west side of the village: "Great places for a child to play."

Getting ready for a jaunt from Tonderghie Row

But Douglas also remembered the days when the harbour was not the bustling place it is today: "It was very run down, with the end of the pier damaged and unusable. Some of the trading schooners came and went mainly under auxiliary power and there was the odd steamer bringing coal. There were very few local boats of any kind."

Architecturally the village changed little in the last century. A few gaps appeared where old houses were pulled down. But post-war social housing changed the scene with two major schemes. Since then the Loreburn Housing Association have also helped – but not solved – the problem of homes for local people.

There has also been considerable, if sporadic, building in the private sector at Rosie's Brae and elsewhere, but probably the most significant development is the continuing change on the harbour frontage.

13 – Faith Runs Deep...

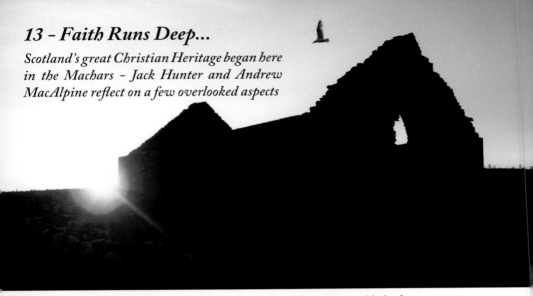

13 – Faith Runs Deep...

Scotland's great Christian Heritage began here in the Machars – Jack Hunter and Andrew MacAlpine reflect on a few overlooked aspects

Scotland's first Christian missionary, St. Ninian, established his base in the Whithorn area in the mid-fifth century and Isle of Whithorn was for long a contender for its location. A twelfth century biography of the saint described the topography round his famous church, *Candida Casa*, and the description seemed to fit the Isle perfectly. However the series of excavations by Peter Hill between 1984 and 1991 conclusively established Whithorn as the location of *Candida Casa* and its associated religious community. So has the Isle any connection with the great man?

The answer is very probably "Yes". It has been claimed that in the sixth century a religious site was established from Ireland in the area where the ruined chapel, locally known as St Ninian's Chapel, now stands at the north end of the promontory. It would have been created because of the fame of nearby Whithorn as a religious centre and seat of learning and consequently the number of people from Ireland landing here to visit Whithorn. The site may have consisted of a small, wooden chapel with a modest hut for the resident cleric together with a graveyard for local Christians. And the evidence? It is slight indeed: possible traces of an oval-shaped bank surrounding the site of St Ninian's Chapel and its rectangular enclosure. No excavation has been done to test the theory although in 1948 the area further up the hill nearer the village was the subject of an archaeological dig, which yielded nothing.

The first really hard evidence of a Ninianic link dates from the twelfth century and consists of foundations, excavated in 1949, of an earlier building under the remains of the ruined chapel.

It probably had the same function and raison d'être as the latter, which dates from the thirteenth century. It is likely that both buildings were built for the use of pilgrims to St Ninian's shrine who arrived by sea, as large numbers did. They may also have been built to mark the traditional spot where the saint first came ashore. It has been suggested from the location that one or both of them may have served also as a lighthouse, providing pilgrims with both physical and spiritual light and guidance. Portpatrick furnishes an example of such a dual-purpose building.

If all this is an inadequate consolation prize, it is worth remembering that because no definite traces of a building contemporary with St Ninian have been found at the Isle, that does not mean that they do not exist. The Steam Packet Inn may one day have a rival as the village's most celebrated building.

"But why was it built there"? This is one of the most common questions asked by visitors to the Isle concerning the church. They might also ask if there is any particular significance in the prominently displayed date of 1844 above the door.

The story is worth retelling especially as what one writer has called "the most important event in the history of nineteenth-century Scotland" is now largely forgotten.

In 1843 there occurred the Disruption of the Church of Scotland. At that time 'patrons', who were usually local landowners, had the right to appoint ministers to parishes even against the wishes of the congregations involved.

The Isle Church

Popular feeling against this power came to a head in that year when hundreds of Church of Scotland ministers resigned, giving up their churches, manses and stipends. They immediately formed the Free Church of Scotland leaving the established church to be derided by one wit as

> *"The auld Kirk, the cauld Kirk*
> *The Kirk wi'oot the people."*

In an extraordinary burst of popular enthusiasm huge sums of money were raised and over 700 churches were built as well as manses and schools. However, a problem faced some Free Church congregations: local landowners refused to allow churches to be built on ground they controlled. In Argyll the congregation at Strontian hit on the novel idea of a floating iron church and had one built on the Clyde and towed up Loch Sunart, where it remained in use for over twenty years.

It may well be that the Free Church congregation in the Isle faced the same sort of difficulties and solved them by building their church out into the bay, below the high water line, and beyond the control of any landowner.

Harbour Praise - each August, an annual gathering, accompanied by the Creetown Silver Band

The rift between the two churches was finally healed in 1929 when they united. But from all the turmoil of 1843 the Isle gained its most unique building which, indeed at the top of especially high tides seems, like the Strontian church, to be floating in the sea.

Summer
residents at
Harbour House

14 - Feathers and Flowers

Andrew MacAlpine spends a little time watching and waiting...

One feature of the Isle that is overlooked occasionally is the tremendous variety of bird life. At high tide, just beyond the bridge, little flocks of turnstones can be observed from a distance of a couple of yards as, true to their name, they scuttle about flipping over pebbles and fronds of seaweed. Often with them are redshanks, daintily picking their way around the rocks.

At low tide, looking out to the shoreline beyond the harbour, there are oystercatchers and curlews.

Often in the early morning, there are silent, motionless herons. Beyond them, perched on rocks, stand cormorants hanging their wings out to dry. In summertime the screaming terns will be back, plunging into the bay in search of sand eels, while further out gannets will be employing the same method of fishing on a grander scale.

Above: an oystercatcher keeps careful watch, while a heron patrols the rocky shoreline.

The raucous noise of crows comes from Knockanharrie wood just over the water from the harbour. Not glamorous birds, crows - but when they take to the air in their hundreds and swirl about in great flocks performing extraordinary aerobatics it is an astonishing sight.

From the middle of April the swallows and martins, which very sensibly have spent winter south of the Sahara, will begin to return and then we shall know that summer is not far away. These are perhaps the most photographed birds in the Isle, with families of swallows jammed into their little mud nests often to be seen under the eaves of houses. Sometimes these nests may be little more than at head-height, neither adult birds nor fledglings seeming in the least bit disturbed by all the attention they get.

Of course, there are many other species that, with a bit more patience, you may be able to spot around here. A half hour or so spent on the Cairn will usually bring the reward of a bird of prey hovering and waiting, and any walk on the cliff paths may bring a host of seabirds and other sightings.

For those willing to make a little effort there are lots of treats in store just outside the village. A short distance up the road to Burrowhead, skylarks can be heard with their endless song, but to spot them is quite another matter. There is another elusive little bird at the side of the same road. A real fidget, it flits about invisibly in the whins making a big noise but, just for a second, it may perch in full view to reveal its distinctive white throat from which it gets its name.

Fortunately, other small birds are not so shy. Flocks of goldfinches dazzle with their bright colours and linnets can be seen almost right up to Burrowhead. A really bold, cheeky chappie may be seen by the path up to Stein. His black head gives him away as a stonechat.

The biggest thrill, however, probably comes with a sighting of one or other of the various raptors. Kestrels handily hover close above roads and buzzards perch on fence posts and telephone poles. Keep a good look out for a merlin, flying low and fast and, near Dinnans farm, a hen harrier unmistakable with its black wingtips. A bird table set out with goodies for small birds can attract the attention of sparrowhawks as several locals will testify. And then there is the peregrine, which is evidently making a comeback. If you are lucky you may see it on the cliffs. It is a fearsomely efficient hunter able to outpace and knock down the fastest of birds, a fact which does not endear it to pigeon enthusiasts.

Top row: crow and buzzard in mid-air conversation ; an arctic tern over the Harbour bay; sandpiper courtship;
Centre row: kestrel on watch; yellowhammer on dyke;
Bottom row: greedy goldfinches; suppertime for a young starling

Another way of recharging your batteries is to search out the Isle's profusion of wild flowers. It all begins in late January with great drifts of snowdrops, which are to be seen at their best around Glasserton, and further afield at Galloway House. Recently there has been correspondence in the local press recalling the days when snowdrops were something of a commercial crop. Long stemmed flowers were chosen and tied up in large bunches decorated with ivy leaves. Boxes of ten dozen bunches each were sent by overnight train from Newton Stewart to London. Cold and finicky work but profitable until transport costs rose and fashions changed.

Winter's afternoon in Galloway House Gardens

Head for the cliffs along the coastal walk between Burrowhead and St Ninian's Cave to see masses of blue spring squills (photo p34) and the shining yellow of the primrose. It seems extraordinary that they should thrive in such wind-blasted places and, in the case of the primrose, often on virtually sunless slopes. In the past the primrose was valued as an herbal remedy to 'purge the heid', which sounds useful as a cure for the effects of over-indulgence. An old Scots recipe called for the juice of the primrose to be mixed with milk and then, with a straw, blown up the nose. It sounds fairly drastic, but a lot more exciting than swallowing a pill! No doubt the shock of such a treatment did indeed clear the head.

Gorse, or whins, can provide a welcome splash of colour right through the winter months

-124-

Spring in Physgill Glen   As the first leaves appear on the trees come the bluebells.   One of the more picturesque old Scots names for it was 'gowk's hose', which translates as cuckoo's socks.   The calls of the first cuckoo in spring coincided with the blue smoke of massed bluebells.   Few wild flowers can rival the sight of carpets of bluebells in a wood lit by shafts of sunlight.   And where better to see them than in Physgill Glen?

Summer is just round the corner when the sea pinks appear. Sea campion shelters below.

The Isle of Whithorn has been singularly successful in its bids for regional and national funding as well as wider recognition of its efforts on behalf of the community

Local Politics - *by Jean Marshall*

The village has always been at the forefront of local political management. Long before the setting up of the statutory body of the Community Council, the village had its own very efficient Village Improvements Committee, set up just after the war. It became very successful in getting things done for the village, s o much so that when the statutory body was introduced and neighbouring Whithorn wanted the Isle to come under its wing there was very vigorous protest from the community who believed that the Isle's problems were very different. Time has proved them right.

Today's Community Council has striven to deal with many concerns affecting the area.

Above: the Village Improvements Committee meets in 1974; a meeting of the Community Council in 2004

Since 2000 there's been much hard work collaborating with the community charity Isle Futures on regeneration projects – including a new slipway and its eventual handover to Dumfries & Galloway Council. In 2008 it jointly negotiated the management takeover of St. Ninian's Hall and, as part of the process, successfully reversed the closure of public toilet facilities.

A major feature of the Community Council's work has been the continual lobbying of local authority, agencies and individuals to assist the Isle's progress. Sometimes the work has been consultative – such as the development of coastal paths around the south of the Machars peninsula, or pressing for road safety measures in the village such as chicanes, speed checks and location of bus stops.

Occasionally, representations are made on planning applications made in this designated Outstanding Conservation Area and Site of Special Scientific Interest.

Storm, sewage and potential flooding issues have involved frequent dialogue with Scottish Water, SEPA and the local authority, as have the works to reinforce and underground power supplies. The Community Council closely monitors the provision of public services – grass cutting, street cleaning and maintenance, refuse bin emptying and beach cleans, road signage, recycling collection points, sandbags for flood prevention, street lighting and the upkeep of bus shelters.

Flooding in February 2001 was caused by a combination of high spring tides and a period of southerly gales

New stage lighting for the Village Hall was made possible by awards from the Calor Scottish Community of the Year contest

Liaison with the Police is excellent, with representation on their Committee, as well as on the Board of Machars Action. Besides the monthly meetings, members regularly attend the Wigtown Area Committee sessions, which enable them to bring up issues directly with councillors. Several grants have been received from this Committee in connection with community events and in support of Christmas lighting.

Partnership working has been a hallmark of many of the activities – with Dumfries and Galloway Council in the provision of new paths, the provision of additional car parking and boat storage areas, as well as pavement and road repairs.

To spread the workload on the Community Council, several sub-groups report to the main Council on a monthly basis: Isle in Bloom the Gala Committee and the Youngsters' Project Group, which provides many opportunities for youngsters, and a Housing Group which successfully progressed the Isle's bid for affordable housing.

In recognition of the efforts of the many small groups and associations in and around the village, the Community Council received major awards (Calor Scotland 2003 & 2004), including a Civic Reception by Dumfries & Galloway Council. Prize monies from these awards were used to install new sound and stage lighting in St Ninian's Hall. The Community Council successfully pushed for the formation of a First Response Team, (see page 144 in this chapter).

The generosity of residents and friends has greatly assisted the Isle's fundraising efforts. It is thanks to them that several new seats have been placed around the Cairn, a new community notice board and 'Welcome' sign have been placed in the village. Generous donations from Isle Futures, private donors and the Community Council have enabled events such as the annual fireworks display to take place. In a typical year, this small community had raised over £25,000 for various groups in the Isle as well as outside charities.

Even more lobbying took place to keep the Isle's Post Office open. It plays a vital role in village life, and it was with much relief that it escaped the 2009 round of Post Office closures. Improvements to the telephone network, broadband connectivity and mobile phone coverage continue to be sought.

A new Community Council was elected at the end of 2009, and they will be continuing with the hard work that ensures the Isle remains a vibrant community, with a strong voice and desire to maintain the level of success that has already been achieved.

Activities at the Cairn: the Community Council is presented with a new seat by a descendant of an Isle family; and the popular annual fireworks display.

Isle Futures - *Improving the economic, social and environmental life of the Isle of Whithorn - by Ian Duncanson*

Isle Futures was set up in late 2001 charged with the task of addressing the needs of the community, and to act as its collective voice in obtaining funding and other support from local, regional and national agencies for economic, social and environmental benefit and improvement. This community-led company, limited by guarantee, became a Registered Charity in 2006 with a Board of Trustees, and now has over 300 Members resident in the Isle, or who live elsewhere and have expressed an interest in the community's progress.

The new slipway now provides easy access for craft at all states of the tide.

The current mainstay of the village, with regards to employment and income, is tourism. One of the first projects undertaken was a feasibility study in 2001 into the improvement of Harbour Row and the provision of a new slipway. The slipway would provide better access at all states of the tide and its construction was completed in 2002. That same year, a detailed Community Survey was undertaken where every household in the Isle and surrounding area was asked for its views on a broad range of topics - transport, accessibility to services, health, employment etc. The information collected was used to further develop a Regeneration Programme, and provide evidence of the community's wishes when applying for funding. The survey indicated that a facility such as a One Stop Shop would enable local people to have better access to services such as learning opportunities, leisure courses and business support services, and even provide a small retail outlet.

Over the next year and a half, funding grants from Scottish Enterprise, Dumfries & Galloway Council, the European LEADER + Programme and the Quality of Life Fund enabled progress to be made with an extensive programme of research and development work. Funding was obtained for a Business Plan to include the new slipway, marketing and a small amount of staff support to undertake projects supplying training, IT, marketing and finance skills for new tourism and business start-ups.

The Wigtown Area Council Committee gave early funding support for events such as the Isle Hamefairin', an important event for marketing and for promoting the Isle.

The efforts and achievements of the community were recognised in a number of National awards. In 2003 the Isle was the Calor Scotland Community Life Winner and runner-up for Business. Powell Publishing's Community Fundraising Award soon followed, and in 2004 there was further success with the Isle of Whithorn becoming the Calor Scottish Community of the Year.

That same year, an ambitious project began to gather historic material to create 'Isle Heritage'. Several exhibitions have

Below: The first Isle Heritage exhibition in 2003; and the very successful Art exhibition held in the Isle Church in 2008

been held, featuring the community's involvement with the land and the sea, and specific periods such as the wartime years at the Isle. Exhibitions like these brought in increased numbers of visitors to the Isle Church and a substantial sum in donations towards its upkeep.

In July 2008, the Isle Church was home to an art exhibition with the artist donating a large proportion of the profits to the church restoration fund and the village hall restoration fund. This demonstrated that the building had considerable potential for appropriate events in the future. Isle Futures has provided funding assistance to improve the vestry, with a new toilet and small kitchen facility.

Above: The Village Hall in 2001.

Following community takeover in 2008, teams of volunteers have undertaken an immense amount of renovation work.

A further feasibility study undertaken into the viability for a One Stop Shop concluded in 2005 that there was scope to develop outreach services from St. Ninian's Hall, as well as managing the hall and piloting a community café/retail outlet. However, the likely £35,000 cost of bringing the building into an acceptable state of repair was considered a major stumbling block. With no Council funding available for this work in the foreseeable future, and the likelihood of the hall becoming unusable within a few years, Isle Futures and the Isle of Whithorn Community Council convened a Joint Strategy Group to consider the options and begin a community consultation process. Public meetings and a postal survey of residents took place and there was overwhelming support in favour of negotiating a contract for the community to take over the management of St. Ninian's Hall. Such is the way that funding from public sources is organised that this arrangement effectively unlocked finance from other budgets within the local authority as well as other agencies!

Since August 2008, St. Ninian's Hall has been managed by the community, and significant progress has been made with refurbishment. Urgent repairs, external and interior decorating were undertaken, new seating, staging, additional stage lighting and more efficient heating and lighting systems have been installed. The public toilets adjacent to the Hall that were under threat of closure were included within the lease contract.

Isle Futures, as the community's regeneration charity, has over the years supported a series of events in partnership with community organisations and local businesses. The extremely popular Isle Hamefairin' has now become the premier annual food and craft event in the Machars, and provides local produce and craft businesses with sales and marketing opportunities. In recent years the event has been entirely self-funded and is very dependent on local volunteers to ensure its continued success.

The charity has provided support within the community to the Gala Committee, Youngsters' Projects Group, Isle Bowling Club, and Wigtown Bay Sailing Club for sail training for youngsters, as well as the village Fireworks Display and the Machars Movies film group.

A successful funding bid was made to Scottish Screen for the purchase and installation of digital cinema equipment enabling a community cinema to be established in St. Ninian's Hall. A further bid to the Scottish Arts Council enabled the provision of improved staging and lighting - new facilities which will be important in promoting the venue for business events, meetings and social functions.

The continuing progress of the community on these projects together with the Annual Report of the Isle Futures Charity can be found on the Isle's website at www.isleofwhithorn.com

Opposite: Isle Hamefairin' events have been held regularly since 2001

Isle Hamefairin' - *by Judy Brown*

As the foot & mouth disease outbreak in 2001 began to show signs of abating, a small group began to work on an idea for an event that would give the local community something positive to look forward to.

Simply called *The Isle Event* it was to be a celebration of the very best in local food and farming, as well as fishing, crafts and heritage, all wrapped up with music and plenty of fun. An enthusiastic team quickly set to work.

First task – to raise finance - and many sponsors and private individuals rallied to the cause. Exhibitors were contacted and encouraged to participate.

Brightly coloured market stalls lined the harbour where butchers, bakers and candlemakers, with many other enterprises, were keen to exhibit their wares.

A Community with Spirit...

Local women demonstrated their talents in floral artistry in the Isle Church. There were cookery and craft demonstrations while afternoon teas satisfied many of the two thousand visitors who thronged the Isle.

An air-sea rescue exercise involving two lifeboats and a Royal Navy helicopter provided a dramatic finale. The seeds had been sown for a community-run event that is now an established part of the local calendar.

From a Food & Seafood Festival to the Isle Hamefairin', as it is now known, the event has gone from strength to strength, sometimes despite the vagaries of weather.

Several of our regular exhibitors have become close friends with the team of volunteers at the Isle.

Exhibitor or visitor, many even plan their holidays to coincide with the Hamefairin'! Such is our reputation for good organisation, friendly atmosphere and maintaining high standards.

The organisers of the Hamefairin' owe a huge debt of gratitude to the large number of volunteers who give their time, talents and enthusiasm to make this event a success each year.

Opposite: The Village Hall in August 2009, and a few more of the volunteers who worked tirelessly on the project.

St Ninian's Hall - The Meeting Place - *by Bob Rowley*

A village hall – the heart of any small community - a place where local people can get together... a place for meetings, social gatherings, parties, dances, pantomimes, and much more...

This nineteen thirties building has seen a lot of comings and goings over the years. Early records are hard to come by, but one villager remembers her mother describing how the community raised the money to build the hall. At the beginning of 1930, the Womens' Rural first met there, and paid the Hall Secretary and Treasurer (then Mr Curran, who ran the Post Office) a year's rent of 45 shillings (£2.25). During this time the Rural also donated money towards the installation of electricity (complete with meters) in the hall, and it also paid £12.7s.7d (£12.38) for curtains and fittings. Through the years, the Rural's many contributions to the maintenance and fabric of the building continued – piano, cooker, water urns, as well as the making and cleaning of stage curtains.

The rent was paid to hall trustees and a part of this was used to pay the hallkeeper - often 30% or more of the rental cost. From 1955 onwards the charge for hall and hallkeeper appeared to be combined, this suggesting that the Council may by then have taken over the premises.

Weddings and parties, concerts, plays, youngsters' activities and public meetings (one session in October 1991 to debate power cuts in village and surroundings saw the hall packed to standing room only), as well as being a polling station have all added to the variety of purposes in what has become a much loved and used building in the community.

The hall was closed for several months at the beginning of 1992 for renovations, including a new floor. During this time, the Wigtown Bay Sailing Club provided a very useful, if smaller, alternative venue.

Under the control of Dumfries & Galloway Council, there was never much money available to put towards maintenance, and the building began to take on a somewhat run-down look. Despite this, the Isle's successes in the Calor Scottish Community of the Year Awards gave us a boost with prize money to install sound and stage lighting facilities.

It took nearly three years of protracted negotiations to prepare a lease agreement between the community and the Council so that we could begin to manage the premises ourselves. The Hall Management Committee, made up of representatives from all user groups in the village, together with many other volunteers, put in hundreds of hours of hard work, completely refurbishing the hall.

Now, St. Ninian's Hall has become 'the place to be' for a whole range of activities - theatre, music, exhibitions, parties and receptions. It's now home to Scotland's most southerly cinema! And of course, it remains the heart of the village. Another example of this little community that is determined to succeed.

How the Silver Screen came to the Isle - *by Mike Marshall*

There are still a few villagers who remember the last time a cinema operated in the Isle, in the Second World War, when the village hall hosted film shows for the many hundreds of service personnel based in the area. A projector would be set up in the ladies toilet, and a small hole in the wall enabled the film to be beamed onto a screen at the other end of the hall!

So, could cinema enjoy a renaissance here at the Isle some sixty years later?

Elsewhere in this chapter you will read how the Isle decided to push forward with community regeneration, and that one of the most challenging projects has been the taking over of its most precious asset – the village hall. Halls are a bit like trains or buses. They have to run, regardless of whether there are passengers to fill the seats. An empty hall, no matter how comfortable, doesn't pay the electricity and the water bills, meet the cost of repairs, the insurance premiums or the licences required for a place of entertainment.

Finding an activity that could provide a regular flow of income, as well as enhance the social function of the building posed us all with a particular challenge.

St Ninian's Hall today - a versatile and increasingly popular venue in the Machars peninsula

Our bigger vision did not escape the attention of the creative arts agency Scottish Screen. Bringing the cinema to remote rural areas of Scotland is one of their major remits. Their digital projection equipment fund enabled state-of-the-art technology to be installed at St. Ninian's Hall, and since May 2009 the Isle has become the location of Scotland's most southerly cinema.

Machars Movies is the name of the volunteer-led organisation that's responsible for a regular programme of films. It draws on a very focused and supportive membership who come from as far afield as Glenluce, Wigtown and Newton Stewart, and the closer communities of Garlieston, Sorbie, Port William and Whithorn, as well as the Isle. It provides a much looked-forward to and hugely social experience for residents and visitors to the area. Occasionally, evenings have been held as 'Themed Nights', with catering to suit, and the 'House Full' sign is frequently displayed for these. The films are chosen by popular vote, and include classic as well as contemporary cinema, documentary, foreign language and world cinema titles. It helps other organisations and groups hold their own film shows, and the cinema becomes a screening venue for other arts events in Dumfries & Galloway, notably the Wigtown Booktown Festival, and the Dumfries Film Festival.

In 2010, the enterprise shown by Machars Movies, working in conjunction with the St. Ninian's Hall Management team and the community regeneration company Isle Futures, was recognised at both National and UK level by the Scottish Countryside Alliance and the Countryside Alliance respectively with the Award 'Best Rural Enterprise'.

Isle in Bloom - Blooming Marvellous - *by Norma Whitton*

With much of the Isle designated an Outstanding Conservation Area, it's right and proper that the community does all it can to maintain that image.

That was the philosophy of the Community Council in 2001, which led to the formation of Isle in Bloom. Over the following eight years volunteers weeded and planted, tidied and painted, raised money and ran competitions, and occasionally stood up to Dumfries & Galloway Council when it was considered we weren't receiving our fair share of support in essential environmental maintenance.

Planters were sited and flower beds created with spring, summer and autumn displays throughout the village.

The Witness Cairn, a much loved area, was always weeded and made to look tidy in time for the Easter Sunday Morning Services.

Garden competitions were organised – with a range of categories that covered differing age groups and gardening conditions. The youngsters wanted to join in so they had a Sunflower competition to grow the tallest specimen. Prize monies and funds for the purchase of plants and compost were raised mainly by unique Garden Shed Sales. Appeals were made for the unwanted contents of sheds, garages and greenhouses. Together with sponsorship specifically for the competition expenses, these events funded the group's activities. It was true that someone's rubbish is someone else's treasure!

Sadly, by 2009 the number of able-bodied green-fingered volunteers had dwindled, so Isle in Bloom has now put away its watering hoses and gardening tools.

Maybe one day it will burst into life once more, but even if the group is not regenerated, their eight years of commitment have left a lasting legacy to the Isle in the form of masses of daffodils which flower every Spring.

First Response Team - *by Norma Whitton*

The Isle's remote location presents a number of challenges, especially in terms of response time by the emergency services. Residents in the community are more than 30 miles from the nearest hospital Accident & Emergency Department. An ambulance may take up to an hour to reach a casualty, and in the case of a cardiac arrest, the earlier a victim receives treatment, the better. This is why a locally based First Response Team would be able to provide vital patient support within 8 minutes, thus saving valuable time and, hopefully, a life.

A Junior First Response Team has been set up, with the hope that some will eventually join the main team.

In early 2004, the Isle's Community Council called a meeting to discuss the formation of a First Response Team for the Isle of Whithorn. Some forty people attended, and they heard a Scottish Ambulance Service officer explain how such a team could benefit the community. They learned that two basic elements were needed for such a service – volunteers and the funds to purchase equipment, including a defibrillator. By the end of that meeting, not only had sufficient people volunteered to enable a Team be formed, but promises of money had been made, including one generous donation of £1,000. Over the next three months, the astonishing sum of over £10,200 was raised.

Eight volunteers were trained, with a further six awaiting training. Just over six months after the first public meeting, the Team 'went live'. Two Responders are on call between 7pm and 7am, Monday to Friday. There have always been hopes to enlarge the team to give greater coverage, but being a small and ageing community does make makes further recruitment difficult.

The Isle community consistently achieves very high responses to fundraising efforts for many local and national charities

The Isle Gala - *by Marion Sunderland & Hayley Gamble*

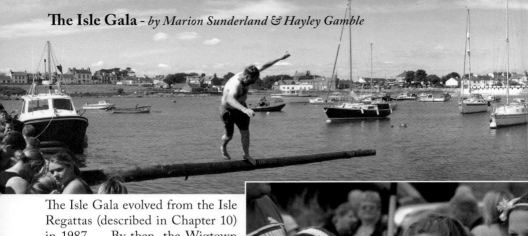

The Isle Gala evolved from the Isle Regattas (described in Chapter 10) in 1987. By then, the Wigtown Bay Sailing Club found that it was no longer able to run the Regattas, with its events of rowing, swimming, and the famous greasy pole. Marion Sunderland who had been a past winner of all these three events, volunteered to take over the task, and it became the Isle Gala Day. Effectively, it meant starting from scratch – there were no grants or sponsorships. Marion approached local businesses asking them for donations, and her mother, the retired Head Teacher of the Isle School, rattled a collection can up and down the harbour to raise funds.

Entertainment was provided by the Garlieston Pipe Band and a group of young Scottish Country Dancers from the Isle that included Anys Scoular, Hayley Gamble, Elizabeth and Margaret Flannigan and Claire Vance. There were several Gala dances on the Saturday night.

Others eventually took over the organisation and the Isle Gala has gone from strength to strength.

At one time there were events throughout an entire week, but now it has reverted to two days with a variety of different events such as parades of floats and fancy dress, along with a fairground. Many hundreds of people come to the village and the harbour for the annual summer spectacle of fun and frolics. The one event constant from the beginning has been the greasy pole, and it appears to grow in popularity every year with as many as 40 people taking part.

For the Isle, the Gala and Regatta are part of our heritage and events we remember with pride.

In 2009, the Gala Committee re-introduced a few of the water sports from years gone by, such as the two-oared race and the outboard engine race. Some of the participants from the earlier days of the Regatta were more than happy to get out there again to take part, along with others, much to the delight of the crowds on the harbour.

Young and old alike look forward to the event each year and as a village we are endeavouring to make sure it remains a highlight – weather permitting!

Isle Old Folks' Committee

The late Charlie Fox (seen on the left with another local worthy, Charlie McGuire) was a Lancastrian engineer who in the sixties started to spend most of his holidays in the village. He was a keen angler – and eventually bought a share in a well known fishing and sea angling boat, *Workmaid*.

As retirement drew near Charlie resolved to make his permanent home in the village and was in fact the first resident to move into Laigh Isle. Outside was a large notice – *Chateau Indubitably* – his own way of poking gentle fun at himself, for the latter word in the title was his favourite as an evening progressed – and maybe his own personal test of sobriety. Unfortunately a very serious car accident, for which he was not to blame, left Charlie with serious injuries and his much planned for retirement was neither as long nor as happy as he would have wished. After a long and painful spell of ill health, the village learned he had left most of his estate to be used for the benefit of the older and needy folk in the village as a thank-you for the kindness the people of the community had shown him. A local committee of Trustees work with the village's Old Folks' Committee, and Christmas-time has always brought the elderly a generous gift towards seasonal cheer – long may the villagers live to give thanks and enjoy Charlie's parting gesture.

A Christmas gathering for the Isle's older folk in 2003

A dramatic picture taken from the Cairn as two club cruisers storm out on a race to Ross Island

Wigtown Bay Sailing Club - *by John Scoular & Norma Whitton*

1955 to 2010 – over fifty years down tide. Wigtown Bay Sailing Club can certainly look back on an eventful half-century. What started as a simple Club, aiming to look after the interests of local boat owners, whether fishermen or sailors, or merely those who enjoy messing about in boats, has become a much more stable and sophisticated operation.

It's easy to forget that in the 1950's, the harbour and village were almost unrecognisable from what we see today. There was no modern quay or real harbour protection and few boats used the rather delapidated structure. The Club's beginnings were simple. For example, the first launching slipway was built by the Club members themselves, led and directed by the late Donald McGuire, one of the many founders. When the opportunity came up to buy the house, which is now the Club's modern headquarters, it was the local members who dipped into their private resources to fund its purchase.

This theme of self-help has been repeated throughout the Club's history. Money raised locally, together with an occasional grant has, over the years, helped to enhance the Club's equipment and bring the clubhouse up to modern day standards.

In the Club's earlier days, one big leap forward in sailing terms came when members agreed the G. P. 14 racing dinghy was ideal for local conditions. In those days the Club took a team around

Keeping up with time-honoured traditions - restoring the *D F Fisher,* a simple rowing boat that's been at the Isle since 1940.

to other local sailing venues – Kippford, Lochryan, Lochmaben and Kirkcudbright. They transported the boats on an iron frame, which fitted neatly on top of Gavie Cronie's coal lorry. Care was needed to remember to lash everything down as low as possible to pass under the then Kirkinner railway bridge.

elping people to learn to sail, or make the best and safest use of their craft, has always been a major part of the Club's activities.

If our Club members travelled, so too did those from elsewhere – coming to the Isle to support our regattas and other events. It was not uncommon for the clubhouse to become temporary overnight accommodation. For years the Club ran the traditional regattas, with their popular programme of greasy pole, swimming and the hotly contested outboard motor race. Now, these water sports are organised by the Isle's Gala Committee.

Today, the Club holds specific fund-raising activities to send youngsters and adults to local sail training schools where they gain RYA Certificates of Competence.

The clubhouse itself is an important part of the whole community. It's available as a meeting place or a venue for fund-raising events and offers changing and shower facilities for visiting and local sailors. Its up-to-date interior is also home to a rich variety of antiques and memorabilia which show a maritime history going back well before the Club came into existence.

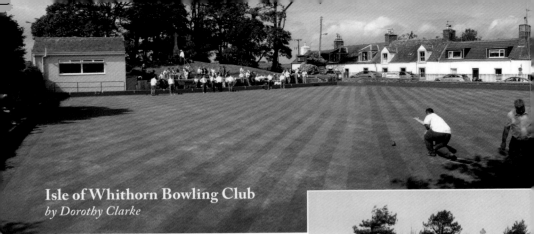

Isle of Whithorn Bowling Club
by Dorothy Clarke

It was in June 1894 that a group of eleven people got together to form the Isle's Bowling Club. In February 1896, a Mr. John McWilliam offered to erect a clubhouse at his own expense. The cost was £29.13s.0d! (£29.65).

In 1989 the Club won the Galloway Estates Cup for the first time in 80 years. A year later, planning consent was sought to demolish the old building and erect a new clubhouse with catering and toilet facilities. Three years later, the new building was complete and a cheese & wine evening was held to celebrate the Official Opening.

The original foundation stone from the end of the old building can now be seen in the wall facing the Green just along from the new clubhouse.

The Club has been successful in recent years – winning the Machars Men's League in 1993, as well as the Galloway Estate Cup for a second time in 1994. The Ladies section also has a team playing in the Wigtownshire League, and has done well over the years, winning the Machars League in 1998.

In 1996, our Centenary Year, Isle of Whithorn (also known as "The Seagulls") won both the Stair and Monreith Cups. The local paper described this as a remarkable achievement for such a small but dedicated Club.

Above: The Club today and pictured in the 1920's; a gathering of players caught on camera about 1910; Wigtownshire League Ladies Champions team 2005

The Isle Rural - *by Dorothy McIlwraith*

The 39 ladies who attended a meeting in the Isle school in October 1923 could never have imagined that they were about to start a branch of an organisation which has met regularly ever since. With many of them paying a membership subscription of two shillings and one penny (just over 10p in today's money) the Isle of Whithorn branch of the Scottish Womens Rural Institute was formed.

The first President was Mrs Brown, Cutreoch, with Mrs Palmer, Boyach, as Vice-President. The Secretary was Miss Fleetwood who gave her address as The White Lodge, Isle of Whithorn. The Treasurer was Miss Carmichael, the schoolmistress. The Rural flourished - by 1930 there were 99 members, and 108 in 1939. Sadly the original Minute Book has been lost, but Miss Carmichael kept meticulous books which give a real insight into life in the village at that time. Demonstrators were often met off the train at Whithorn and either given hospitality for the night or stayed at the Queens Arms at a cost of 8/- (40p) for supper, bed and breakfast. A bargain surely as the bus fare to Stranraer was 6/6d (32.5p) and car hires were 12/- (60p) from the Isle to Monreith!

For the first few years, the school cleaner, Mrs McCubbin was paid 2/6d (12.5p) per night and coal at 2/6d per cwt and oil at 1/1d (5.5p) per gallon were purchased for heating and lighting.

By 1930, meetings were held in the Public Hall where the Rural still meets. The members really enjoyed outings. In 1927, 44 ladies went to Kirkcudbright. By 1931 they had become more adventurous and 45 members paid 4/- (20p) each for a train ticket from Whithorn to Edinburgh.

Then there were whist drives, Burns' suppers and basket teas (when members brought their baskets of dishes and food and they – along with their invited friends – enjoyed entertainment and a dance).

For many years members took their surplus eggs to meetings and these were sent to hospitals in Dumfries and Glasgow.

The Rural was particularly active during the Second World War. In 1940,

an SWRI van was sited in the Isle Farm garden (courtesy of Mr Cummings). This was staffed by a dietician and a gardener who gave lots of advice to the womenfolk of the Isle and surrounding Rurals. Members could apply for sugar for jam-making and wool and material to make items for the Forces and for "American seeds". They also took turns in borrowing a canning machine which moved round the county. Members discussed topics such as fruit bottling, re-footing lisle stockings and making string bags!

Above: a Rural outing, sometime in the 1950's; members enjoying a Burns Supper in 1962

Service personnel who were locally stationed often spoke at meetings and entertained at the many concerts and dances organised by the Rural. In the thirties and forties there were many young members, and there was also a Young Members' Committee. From early days right up to 1986 a Halloween party was arranged for the village children when members provided the food and organised the games.

Moving with the times, the monthly meetings are definitely more relaxed – no more hats, elaborate suppers or the National Anthem - and today's topics such as the Amish people, local history, village quizzes, trying calligraphy, glass painting and pottery seem to appeal more than "Women & Citizenship", "Cleaning and Trussing a Fowl", "Hay Box Cookery" & "How to make Bedroom Slippers out of Old Hats"!

The Rural has provided friendship, education and fun for generations of Isle women, and on the first Monday of each month there is still a warm welcome for members and visitors alike.

Members enjoy the keen competition of the Whithorn Flower Show

The Isle Youngsters - *by Kay Lewis*

Every generation of youngsters in the Isle is important, representing the community's future. They're fortunate in having dedicated volunteers to organise weekly activities for them. Games such as tambourelli play an important part in getting the youngsters to come along, and from time to time during the year they look forward to visits to pantomimes and other places of interest such as Mabie Farm and Cream o'Galloway. Older youngsters have been on study visits to Langholm and New Galloway and also to the Glasgow Science Museum.

They regularly undertake fundraising activities – organising car washes and bingo nights, making gifts and Christmas cards, and running a local Christmas card delivery service. They've regularly helped out with the annual Christmas dinner for older folks in the village, and a few of the older youngsters have taken part in first-aid courses with the Junior First Response team. They have participated in writing articles for the community magazine, *Isle News*, featuring events like Halloween and Bonfire Nights, along with all the fun of the summer Gala days. The vibrancy of the Youngsters' Project Group earned them the Young People's Award in the Calor Scottish Community of the Year contest in 2004.

Several village related projects have been undertaken, starting with two outdoor meeting places or 'pods', designed by the youngsters and built with the help of residents. They successfully persuaded the Police and local Council to provide a kickwall. A new raised planter on the village green was completed with four inspiring mosaic designs depicting the points of the compass. Outside the Isle Post Office is a colourful wrought iron planter portraying various aspects of the Isle, which was designed and made by them in conjunction with metal sculpture artist Rachel McWilliam.

Youth cluster groups in the Machars villages of Port William, Kirkinner, Garlieston and Sorbie, as well as the Isle, have been helped to grow with funding for a youth worker, and this is providing stimulating new opportunities for our youngsters.

Index